CH

ary

U·X·L
ENCYCLOPEDIA OF
LANDFORMS
AND OTHER GEOLOGIC FEATURES

U·X·L
ENCYCLOPEDIA OF
LANDFORMS
AND OTHER GEOLOGIC FEATURES

2

Fault
Floodplain
Geyser and hot spring
Glacial landforms and features
Landslide and other gravity movements
Mesa and butte
Meteorite crater
Mountain

Rob Nagel

U·X·L®

Detroit • New York • San Diego • San Francisco • Cleveland • New Haven, Conn. • Waterville, Maine • London • Munich

THOMSON
GALE

U•X•L Encyclopedia of Landforms and Other Geologic Features
Rob Nagel

Project Editor
Diane Sawinski

Permissions
Lori Hines

Imaging and Multimedia
Robyn Young

Product Design
Michelle DiMercurio

Composition
Evi Seoud

Manufacturing
Rita Wimberley

Library of Congress Cataloging-in-Publication Data
Nagel, Rob.
 UXL encyclopedia of landforms and other geologic features / Rob Nagel.
  p. cm.
   Summary: Explores the physical structure of the Earth's landforms, including what they are, how they look, how they were created and change over time, and major geological events associated with each.
   Includes bibliographical references (p.xxix).
   ISBN 0-7876-7611-X (set hardcover) — ISBN 0-7876-7670-5 (Volume 1) — ISBN 0-7876-7671-3 (Volume 2) — ISBN 0-7876-7672-1 (Volume 3)
   1. Landforms—Encyclopedias, Juvenile. 2. Physical geography—Encyclopedias, Juvenile. [1. Landforms—Encyclopedias. 2. Physical geography—Encyclopedias.] I. Title: Encyclopedia of landforms and other geologic features. II. Title.
 GB406.N35 2003
 551.41′03—dc22
                                                        2003014898

Printed in the United States of America
10 9 8 7 6 5 4 3 2 1

Contents

Reader's Guide

From the perspective of human time, very little changes on the surface of Earth. From the perspective of geologic time, the period from Earth's beginning more than 4.5 billion years ago to the present day, however, the surface of the planet is in constant motion, being reshaped over and over. The constructive and destructive forces at play in this reshaping have helped create landforms, specific geomorphic features on Earth's land surface. Mountains and canyons, plains and plateaus, faults and basins: These are but a few of the varied and spectacular features that define the landscape of the planet.

U•X•L Encyclopedia of Landforms and Other Geologic Features explores twenty-two of these landforms: what they are, how they look, how they were created, how they change over time, and major geological events associated with them.

Scope and Format

In three volumes, *U•X•L Encyclopedia of Landforms and Other Geologic Features* is organized alphabetically into the following chapters:

Basin

Cave

Continental margin

Delta

Fault

Geyser and hot spring

Landslide and other gravity movements

Canyon

Coast and shore

Coral reef

Dune and other desert features

Floodplain

Glacial landforms and features

Mesa and butte

Meteorite crater   Mountain
Ocean basin   Plain
Plateau   Stream and river
Valley   Volcano

Each chapter begins with an overview of that specific landform. The remaining information in the chapter is broken into four sections:

- **The shape of the land** describes the physical aspects of the landform, including its general size, shape, and location on the surface of the planet, if applicable. A standard definition of the landform opens the discussion. If the landform exists as various types, those types are defined and further described.

- **Forces and changes: Construction and destruction** describes in detail the forces and agents responsible for the construction, evolution, and destruction of the landform. The erosional actions of wind and water, the dynamic movement of crustal plates, the influence of gravity, and the changes in climate both across regions and time are explained in this section, depending on their relation to the specific landform.

- **Spotlight on famous forms** describes specific examples of the landform in question. Many of these examples are well-known; others may not be. The biggest, the highest, and the deepest were not the sole criteria for selection, although many of the featured landforms meet these superlatives. While almost all chapters include examples found in the United States, they also contain examples of landforms found throughout the world.

- **For More Information** offers students further sources for research—books or Web sites—about that particular landform.

Other features include more than 120 color photos and illustrations, "Words to Know" boxes providing definitions of terms used in each chapter, sidebar boxes highlighting interesting facts relating to particular landforms, a general bibliography, and a cumulative index offering easy access to all of the subjects discussed in *U•X•L Encyclopedia of Landforms and Other Geologic Features*.

Acknowledgments

A note of appreciation is extended to *U•X•L Encyclopedia of Landforms and Other Geologic Features* advisors, who provided helpful suggestions when this work was in its formative stages:

Chris Cavette, Science Writer, Fremont, California

Mark Crawford, Geologist, Madison, Wisconsin

Elizabeth Jackson, Adams Elementary School, Cary, North Carolina

Kate Plieth, Fitzgerald High School, Warren, Michigan

Susan Spaniol, Hillside Middle School, Farmington Hills, Michigan

The author would like to extend special thanks to geologist and writer Mark Crawford and science writer Chris Cavette for their insightful critiques and comments on the table of contents and on the material in each chapter. The advice of Mr. Crawford, in particular, proved invaluable.

Thanks are also extended to U•X•L publisher Tom Romig and product manager Julia Furtaw for developing this title and offering it to the author. Working with the entire U•X•L staff has always been a distinct pleasure.

Finally, and most important, the author would like to offer warm and gracious thanks to U•X•L senior editor Diane Sawinski. Without her guidance, enthusiasm, and tireless effort, this work would not appear as it does.

Comments and Suggestions

We welcome your comments on *U•X•L Encyclopedia of Landforms and Other Geologic Features*. Please write: Editors, *U•X•L Encyclopedia of Landforms and Other Geologic Features*, U•X•L, 27500 Drake Rd., Farmington Hills, MI 48331; call toll-free: 1-800-877-4253; fax: 248-699-8097; or send e-mail via http://www.gale.com.

Geologic Timescale

Era	Period		Epoch	Started (millions of years ago)
Cenozoic: 66.4 millions of years ago–present time	Quaternary		Holocene	0.01
			Pleistocene	1.6
	Tertiary	Neogene	Pliocene	5.3
			Miocene	23.7
		Paleogene	Oligocene	36.6
			Eocene	57.8
			Paleocene	66.4
Mesozoic: 245–66.4 millions of years ago	Cretaceous		Late	97.5
			Early	144
	Jurassic		Late	163
			Middle	187
			Early	208
	Triassic		Late	230
			Middle	240
			Early	245
Paleozoic: 570–245 millions of years ago	Permian		Late	258
			Early	286
	Carboniferous	Pennsylvanian	Late	320
		Mississippian	Early	360
	Devonian		Late	374
			Middle	387
			Early	408
	Silurian		Late	421
			Early	438
	Ordovician		Late	458
			Middle	478
			Early	505
	Cambrian		Late	523
			Middle	540
			Early	570
Precambrian time: 4500-570 millions of years ago				4500

Words to Know

A

Ablation zone: The area of a glacier where mass is lost through melting or evaporation at a greater rate than snow and ice accumulate.

Abrasion: The erosion or wearing away of bedrock by continuous friction caused by sand or rock fragments in water, wind, and ice.

Abyssal hill: A gently sloping, small hill, typically of volcanic origin, found on an abyssal plain.

Abyssal plain: The relatively flat area of an ocean basin between a continental margin and a mid-ocean ridge.

Accretionary wedge: A mass of sediment and oceanic rock that is transferred from an oceanic plate to the edge of the less dense plate under which it is subducting.

Accumulation zone: The area of a glacier where mass is increased through snowfall at a greater rate than snow and ice is lost through ablation.

Active continental margin: A continental margin that has a very narrow, or even nonexistent, continental shelf and a narrow and steep continental slope that ends in a deep trench instead of a continental rise; it is marked by earthquake and volcanic activity.

Alluvial fan: A fanlike deposit of sediment that forms where an intermittent, yet rapidly flowing canyon or mountain stream spills out onto a plain or relatively flat valley.

Alluvium: A general term for sediment (rock debris such as gravel, sand, silt, and clay) deposited by running water.

Alpine glacier: A relatively small glacier that forms in high elevations near the tops of mountains.

Angle of repose: The steepest angle at which loose material on a slope remains motionless.

Anticline: An upward-curving (convex) fold in rock that resembles an arch.

Arête: A sharp-edged ridge of rock formed between adjacent cirque glaciers.

Arroyo: A steep-sided and flat-bottomed gully in a dry region that is filled with water for a short time only after occasional rains.

Asteroid: A small, irregularly shaped rocky body that orbits the Sun.

Asthenosphere: The section of the mantle immediately beneath the lithosphere that is composed of partially melted rock.

Atmospheric pressure: The pressure exerted by the weight of air over a given area of Earth's surface.

Atoll: A ring-shaped collection of coral reefs that nearly or entirely enclose a lagoon.

B

Back reef: The landward side of a reef between the reefcrest and the land.

Backshore zone: The area of a beach normally affected by waves only during a storm at high tide.

Backswamp: The lower, poorly drained area of a floodplain that retains water.

Backwash: The return flow of water to the ocean following the swash of a wave.

Bajada: Several alluvial fans that have joined together.

Bar: A ridge or mound of sand or gravel that lies underwater a short distance from and parallel to a beach; also commonly known as a sand bar.

Barrier island: A bar that has been built up so that it rises above the normal high tide level.

Barrier reef: A long, narrow ridge of coral relatively near and parallel to a shoreline, separated from it by a lagoon.

Basal sliding: The sliding of a glacier over the ground on a layer of water.

Basalt: A dark, dense volcanic rock, about 50 percent of which is silica.

Base level: The level below which a stream cannot erode.

Basin: A hollow or depression in Earth's surface with no outlet for water.

Bay: A body of water in a curved inlet between headlands.

Beach: A deposit of loose material on shores that is moved by waves, tides, and, sometimes, winds.

Beach drift: The downwind movement of sand along a beach as a result of the zigzag pattern created by swash and backwash.

Bed load: The coarse sediment rolled along the bottom of a river or stream.

Bedrock: The general term for the solid rock that underlies the soil.

Berm: A distinct mound of sand or gravel running parallel to the shoreline that divides the foreshore zone from the backshore zone of a beach.

Blowout: A depression or low spot made in sand or light soil by strong wind.

Bottomset bed: A fine, horizontal layer of clay and silt deposited beyond the edge of a delta.

Breccia: A coarse-grained rock composed of angular, broken rock fragments held together by a mineral cement.

Butte: A flat-topped hill with steep sides that is smaller in area than a mesa.

C

Caldera: Large, usually circular, steep-walled basin at the summit of a volcano.

Canyon: A narrow, deep, rocky, and steep-walled valley carved by a swift-moving river.

Cap rock: Erosion-resistant rock that overlies other layers of less-resistant rock.

Cave: A naturally formed cavity or hollow beneath the surface of Earth that is beyond the zone of light and is large enough to be entered by humans.

Cavern: A large chamber within a cave.

Cave system: A series of caves connected by passages.

Channel: The depression where a stream flows or may flow.

Chemical weathering: The process by which chemical reactions alter the chemical makeup of rocks and minerals.

Cirque: A bowl-shaped depression carved out of a mountain by an alpine glacier.

Cliff: A high, steep face of rock.

Coast: A strip of land that extends landward from the coastline to the first major change in terrain features.

Coastal plain: A low, generally broad plain that lies between an oceanic shore and a higher landform such as a plateau or a mountain range.

Coastline: The boundary between the coast and the shore.

Comet: An icy extraterrestrial object that glows when it approaches the Sun, producing a long, wispy tail that points away from the Sun.

Compression: The reduction in the mass or volume of something by applying pressure.

Continental drift: The hypothesis proposed by Alfred Wegener that the continents are not stationary, but have moved across the surface of Earth over time.

Continental glacier: A glacier that forms over large areas of continents close to the poles.

Continental margin: The submerged outer edge of a continent, composed of the continental shelf and the continental slope.

Continental rise: The gently sloping, smooth-surfaced, thick accumulation of sediment at the base of certain continental slopes.

Continental shelf: The gently sloping region of the continental margin that extends seaward from the shoreline to the continental shelf break.

Continental shelf break: The outer edge of the continental shelf at which there is a sharp drop-off to the steeper continental slope.

Continental slope: The steeply sloping region of the continental margin that extends from the continental shelf break downward to the ocean basin.

Convection current: The circular movement of a gas or liquid between hot and cold areas.

Coral polyp: A small, invertebrate marine animal with tentacles that lives within a hard, cuplike skeleton that it secretes around itself.

Coral reef: A wave-resistant limestone structure produced by living organisms, found principally in shallow, tropical marine waters.

Cordillera: A complex group of mountain ranges, systems, and chains.

Creep: The extremely slow, almost continuous movement of soil and other material downslope.

Crest: The highest point or level; summit.

Crevasse: A deep, nearly vertical crack that develops in the upper portion of glacier ice.

Crust: The thin, solid outermost layer of Earth.

Curtain: A thin, wavy or folded sheetlike mineral deposit that hangs from the ceiling of a cave.

Cut bank: A steep, bare slope formed on the outside of a meander.

D

Debris avalanche: The extremely rapid downward movement of rocks, soil, mud, and other debris mixed with air and water.

Debris flow: A mixture of water and clay, silt, sand, and rock fragments that flows rapidly down steep slopes.

Deflation: The lowering of the land surface due to the removal of fine-grained particles by the wind.

Delta: A body of sediment deposited at the mouth of a river or stream where it enters an ocean or lake.

Desert pavement: Surface of flat desert lands covered with a layer of closely packed coarse pebbles and gravel.

Dip: The measured angle from the horizontal plane (Earth's surface) to a fault plane or bed of rock.

Dissolved load: Dissolved substances, the result of the chemical weathering of rock, that are carried along in a river or stream.

Distributaries: The channels that branch off of the main river in a delta, carrying water and sediment to the delta's edges.

Dune: A mound or ridge of loose, wind-blown sand.

E

Earthflow: The downward movement of water-saturated, clay-rich soil on a moderate slope.

Ecosystem: A system formed by the interaction of a community of plants, animals, and microorganisms with their environment.

Ejecta blanket: The circular layer of rock and dust lying immediately around a meteorite crater.

Emergent coast: A coast in which land formerly under water has gradually risen above sea level through geologic uplift of the land or has been exposed because of a drop in sea level.

Eolian: Formed or deposited by the action of the wind.

Erg: A vast area deeply covered with sand and topped with dunes.

Erosion: The gradual wearing away of Earth surfaces through the action of wind and water.

Erratic: A large boulder that a glacier deposits on a surface made of different rock.

Esker: A long, snakelike ridge of sediment deposited by a stream that ran under or within a glacier.

F

Fall: A sudden, steep drop of rock fragments or debris.

Fall line: The imaginary line that marks the sharp upward slope of land along a coastal plain's inland edge where waterfalls and rapids occur as rivers cross the zone from harder to softer rocks.

Fault: A crack or fracture in Earth's crust along which rock on one side has moved relative to rock on the other.

Fault creep: The slow, continuous movement of crustal blocks along a fault.

Fault line: The line on Earth's surface defining a fault; also known as a fault trace.

Fault plane: The area where crustal blocks meet and move along a fault from the fault line down into the crust.

Fault scarp: A steep-sided ledge or cliff generated as a result of fault movement.

Fault system: A network of connected faults.

Flash flood: A flood that occurs after a period of heavy rain, usually within six hours of the rain event.

Firn: The granular ice formed by the recrystallization of snow; also known as névé.

Fjord: A deep glacial trough submerged with seawater.

Floodplain: An area of nearly flat land bordering a stream or river that is naturally subject to periodic flooding.

Flow: A type of mass wasting that occurs when a loose mixture of debris, water, and air moves down a slope in a fluidlike manner.

Flowstone: The general term for a sheetlike mineral deposit on a wall or floor of a cave.

Fold: A bend or warp in a layered rock.

Foothill: A high hill at the base of a mountain.

Footwall: The crustal block that lies beneath an inclined fault plane.

Fore reef: The seaward edge of a reef that is fairly steep and slopes down to deeper water.

Foreset bed: An inclined layer of sand and gravel deposited along the edge of a delta.

Foreshore zone: The area of a beach between the ordinary low tide mark and the high tide mark.

Fracture zone: The area where faults occur at right angles to a main feature, such as a mid-ocean ridge.

Fringing reef: A coral reef formed close to a shoreline.

Fumarole: A small hole or vent in Earth's surface through which volcanic gases escape from underground.

G

Geyser: A hot spring that periodically erupts through an opening in Earth's surface, spewing hot water and steam.

Geyserite: A white or grayish silica-based deposit formed around hot springs.

Glacial drift: A general term for all material transported and deposited directly by or from glacial ice.

Glacial polish: The smooth and shiny surfaces produced on rocks underneath a glacier by material carried in the base of that glacier.

Glacial surge: The rapid forward movement of a glacier.

Glacial trough: A U-shaped valley carved out of a V-shaped stream valley by a valley glacier.

Glaciation: The transformation of the landscape through the action of glaciers.

Glacier: A large body of ice that formed on land by the compaction and recrystallization of snow, survives year to year, and shows some sign of movement downhill due to gravity.

Graben: A block of Earth's crust dropped downward between faults.

Graded stream: A stream that is maintaining a balance between the processes of erosion and deposition.

Granular flow: A flow that contains up to 20 percent water.

Gravity: The physical force of attraction between any two objects in the universe.

Ground moraine: A continuous layer of till deposited beneath a steadily retreating glacier.

Groundwater: Freshwater lying within the uppermost parts of Earth's crust, filling the pore spaces in soil and fractured rock.

Gully: A channel cut into Earth's surface by running water, especially after a heavy rain.

Guyot: An undersea, flat-topped seamount.

H

Hanging valley: A shallow glacial trough that leads into the side of a larger, main glacial trough.

Hanging wall: The crustal block that lies above an inclined fault plane.

Headland: An elevated area of hard rock that projects out into an ocean or other large body of water.

Hill: A highland that rises up to 1,000 feet (305 meters) above its surroundings, has a rounded top, and is less rugged in outline than a mountain.

Horn: A high mountain peak that forms when the walls of three or more glacial cirques intersect.

Horst: A block of Earth's crust forced upward between faults.

Hot spot: An area beneath Earth's crust where magma currents rise.

Hot spring: A pool of hot water that has seeped through an opening in Earth's surface.

I

Igneous rock: Rock formed by the cooling and hardening of magma, molten rock that is underground (called lava once it reaches Earth's surface).

Internal flow: The movement of ice inside a glacier through the deformation and realignment of ice crystals; also known as creep.

Invertebrates: Animals without backbones.

K

Kame: A steep-sided, conical mound or hill formed of glacial drift that is created when sediment is washed into a depression on the top surface of a glacier and is then deposited on the ground below when the glacier melts away.

Karst topography: A landscape characterized by the presence of sinkholes, caves, springs, and losing streams.

Kettle: A shallow, bowl-shaped depression formed when a large block of glacial ice breaks away from the main glacier and is buried beneath glacial till, then melts. If the depression fills with water, it is known as a kettle lake.

L

Lagoon: A quiet, shallow stretch of water separated from the open sea by an offshore reef or other type of landform.

Lahar: A mudflow composed of volcanic ash, rocks, and water produced by a volcanic eruption.

Landslide: A general term used to describe all relatively rapid forms of mass wasting.

Lateral moraine: A moraine deposited along the side of a valley glacier.

Lava: Magma that has reached Earth's surface.

Lava dome: Mass of lava, created by many individual flows, that forms in the crater of a volcano after a major eruption.

Leeward: On or toward the side facing away from the wind.

Levee (natural): A low ridge or mound along a stream bank, formed by deposits left when floodwater slows down on leaving the channel.

Limestone: A sedimentary rock composed primarily of the mineral calcite (calcium carbonate).

Lithosphere: The rigid uppermost section of the mantle combined with the crust.

Longshore current: An ocean current that flows close and almost parallel to the shoreline and is caused by the angled rush of waves toward the shore.

Longshore drift: The movement of sand and other material along a shoreline in the longshore current.

Losing stream: A stream on Earth's surface that is diverted underground through a sinkhole or a cave.

M

Magma: Molten rock containing particles of mineral grains and dissolved gas that forms deep within Earth.

Magma chamber: A reservoir or cavity beneath Earth's surface containing magma that feeds a volcano.

Mantle: The thick, dense layer of rock that lies beneath Earth's crust.

Mass wasting: The spontaneous movement of material down a slope in response to gravity.

Meander: A bend or loop in a stream's course.

Mechanical weathering: The process by which a rock or mineral is broken down into smaller fragments without altering its chemical makeup.

Medial moraine: A moraine formed when two adjacent glaciers flow into each other and their lateral moraines are caught in the middle of the joined glacier.

Meltwater: The water from melted snow or ice.

Mesa: A flat-topped hill or mountain with steep sides that is smaller in area than a plateau.

Metamorphic rock: Rock whose texture or composition has been changed by extreme heat and pressure.

Meteor: A glowing fragment of extraterrestrial material passing through Earth's atmosphere.

Meteorite: A fragment of extraterrestrial material that strikes the surface of Earth.

Meteorite crater: A crater or depression in the surface of a celestial body caused by the impact of a meteorite; also known as an impact crater.

Meteoroid: A small, solid body floating in space.

Mid-ocean ridge: A long, continuous volcanic mountain range found on the basins of all oceans.

Moraine: The general term for a ridge or mound of till deposited by a glacier.

Mountain: A landmass that rises 1,000 feet (305 meters) or more above its surroundings and has steep sides meeting in a summit that is much narrower in width than the base of the landmass.

Mudflow: A mixture primarily of the smallest silt and clay particles and water that has the consistency of newly mixed concrete and flows quickly down slopes.

Mud pot: A hot spring that contains thick, muddy clay.

O

Oasis: A fertile area in a desert or other dry region where groundwater reaches the surface through springs or wells.

Ocean basin: That part of Earth's surface that extends seaward from a continental margin.

Oxbow lake: A crescent-shaped body of water formed from a single loop that was cut off from a meandering stream.

P

Paleomagnetism. The study of changes in the intensity and direction of Earth's magnetic field through time.

Passive continental margin: A continental margin that has a broad continental shelf, a gentle continental slope, and a pronounced continental rise; it is marked by a lack of earthquake and volcanic activity.

Peneplain: A broad, low, almost featureless surface allegedly created by long-continued erosion.

Photosynthesis: The process by which plants use energy from sunlight to change water and carbon dioxide into sugars and starches.

Piedmont glacier: A valley glacier that flows out of a mountainous area onto a gentle slope or plain and spreads out over the surrounding terrain.

Pinnacle: A tall, slender tower or spire of rock.

Plateau: A relatively level, large expanse of land that rises some 1,500 feet (457 meters) or more above its surroundings and has at least one steep side.

Plates: Large sections of Earth's lithosphere separated by deep fault zones.

Plate tectonics: The geologic theory that Earth's crust is composed of rigid plates that "float" toward or away from each other, either directly or indirectly, shifting continents, forming mountains and new ocean crust, and stimulating volcanic eruptions.

Playa: A shallow, short-lived lake that forms where water drains into a basin and quickly evaporates, leaving a flat surface of clay, silt, and minerals.

Point bar: The low, crescent-shaped deposit of sediment on the inside of a meander.

Pyroclastic material: Rock fragments, crystals, ash, pumice, and glass shards formed by a volcanic explosion or ejection from a volcanic vent.

R

Rapids: The section of a stream where water flows fast over hard rocks.

Reef crest: The high point of a coral reef that is almost always exposed at low tide.

Regolith: The layer of loose, uncemented rocks and rock fragments of various size that lies beneath the soil and above the bedrock.

Rhyolite: A fine-grained type of volcanic rock that has a high silica content.

Rift valley: The deep central crevice in a mid-ocean ridge; also, a valley or trough formed between two normal faults.

Ring of Fire: The name given to the geographically active belt around the Pacific Ocean that is home to more than 75 percent of the planet's volcanoes.

River: A large stream.

Rock flour: Fine-grained rock material produced when a glacier abrades or scrapes rock beneath it.

S

Saltation: The jumping movement of sand caused by the wind.

Sea arch: An arch created by the erosion of weak rock in a sea cliff through wave action.

Seafloor spreading: The process by which new oceanic crust is formed by the upwelling of magma at mid-ocean ridges, resulting in the continuous lateral movement of existing oceanic crust.

Seamount: An isolated volcanic mountain that often rises 3,280 feet (1,000 meters) or more above the surrounding ocean floor.

Sea stack: An isolated column of rock, the eroded remnant of a sea arch, located in the ocean a short distance from the shoreline.

Sediment: Rock debris such as gravel, sand, silt, and clay.

Sedimentary rock: Rock that is formed by the accumulation and compression of sediment, which may consist of rock fragments, remains of microscopic organisms, and minerals.

Shear stress: The force of gravity acting on an object on a slope, pulling it downward in a direction parallel to the slope.

Shock wave: Wave of increased temperature and pressure formed by the sudden compression of the medium through which the wave moves.

Shore: The strip of ground bordering a body of water that is alternately covered or exposed by waves or tides.

Shoreline: The fluctuating line between water and the shore.

Silica: An oxide (a compound of an element and oxygen) found in magma that, when cooled, crystallizes to become the mineral quartz, which is one of the most common compounds found in Earth's crust.

Silt: Fine earthy particles smaller than sand carried by moving water and deposited as a sediment.

Sinkhole: A bowl-like depression that develops on Earth's surface above a cave ceiling that has collapsed or on an area where the underlying sedimentary rock has been eroded away.

Slide: The movement of a mass of rocks or debris down a slope.

Slip face: The steeply sloped side of a dune that faces away from the wind.

Slope failure: A type of mass wasting that occurs when debris moves downward as the result of a sudden failure on a steep slope or cliff.

Slump: The downward movement of blocks of material on a curved surface.

Slurry flow: A flow that contains between 20 and 40 percent water.

Snow line: The elevation above which snow can form and remain all year.

Solifluction: A form of mass wasting that occurs in relatively cold regions in which waterlogged soil flows very slowly down a slope.

Speleothem: A mineral deposit formed in a cave.

Spit: A long, narrow deposit of sand or gravel that projects from land into open water.

Stalactite: An icicle-shaped mineral deposit hanging from the roof of a cave.

Stalagmite: A cone-shaped mineral deposit projecting upward from the floor of a cave.

Strain: The change in a rock's shape or volume (or both) in response to stress.

Strata: The layers in a series of sedimentary rocks.

Stream: Any body of running water that moves downslope under the influence of gravity in a narrow and defined channel on Earth's surface.

Stress: The force acting on an object (per unit of area).

Striations: The long, parallel scratches and grooves produced in rocks underneath a glacier as it moves over them.

Strike: The compass direction of a fault line.

Subduction zone: A region where two plates come together and the edge of one plate slides beneath the other.

Submarine canyon: A steep-walled, V-shaped canyon that is cut into the rocks and sediments of the continental slope and, sometimes, the outer continental shelf.

Submergent coast: A coast in which formerly dry land has been gradually flooded, either by land sinking or by sea level rising.

Surface creep: The rolling and pushing of sand and slightly larger particles by the wind.

Suspended load: The fine-grained sediment that is suspended in the flow of water in a river or stream.

Swash: The rush of water up the shore after the breaking of a wave.

Symbiosis: The close, long-term association between two organisms of different species, which may or may not be beneficial for both organisms.

Syncline: A downward-curving (concave) fold in rock that resembles a trough.

T

Talus: A sloping pile of rock fragments lying at the base of the cliff or steep slope from which they have broken off; also known as scree.

Tarn: A small lake that fills the central depression in a cirque.

Terminal moraine: A moraine found near the terminus of a glacier; also known as an end moraine.

Terminus: The leading edge of a glacier; also known as the glacier snout.

Terrace: The exposed portion of a former floodplain that stands like a flat bench above the outer edges of the new floodplain.

Tide: The periodic rising and falling of water in oceans and other large bodies of water that results from the gravitational attraction of the Moon and the Sun upon Earth.

Till: A random mixture of finely crushed rock, sand, pebbles, and boulders deposited by a glacier.

Tombolo: A mound of sand or other beach material that rises above the water to connect an offshore island to the shore or to another island.

Topset bed: A horizontal layer of coarse sand and gravel deposited on top of a delta.

Travertine: A dense, white deposit formed from calcium carbonate that creates rock formations around hot springs.

Trench: A long, deep, narrow depression on the ocean basin with relatively steep sides.

Turbidity current: A turbulent mixture of water and sediment that flows down a continental slope under the influence of gravity.

U

Uplift: In geology, the slow upward movement of large parts of stable areas of Earth's crust.

U shaped valley: A valley created by glacial erosion that has a profile suggesting the form of the letter "U," characterized by steep sides that may curve inwards at their base and a broad, nearly flat floor.

V

Valley glacier: An alpine glacier flowing downward through a preexisting stream valley.

Ventifact: A stone or bedrock surface that has been shaped or eroded by the wind.

Viscosity: The measure of a fluid's resistance to flow.

Volcano: A vent or hole in Earth's surface through which magma, hot gases, ash, and rock fragments escape from deep inside the planet; the term is also used to describe the cone of erupted material that builds up around that opening.

V-shaped valley: A narrow valley created by the downcutting action of a stream that has a profile suggesting the form of the letter "V," characterized by steeply sloping sides.

W

Waterfall: An often steep drop in a stream bed causing the water in a stream channel to fall vertically or nearly vertically.

Wave crest: The highest part of a wave.

Wave-cut notch: An indentation produced by wave erosion at the base of a sea cliff.

Wave-cut platform: A horizontal bench of rock formed beneath the waves at the base of a sea cliff as it retreats because of wave erosion.

Wave height: The vertical distance between the wave crest and the wave trough.

Wavelength: The horizontal distance between two wave crests or troughs.

Wave trough: The lowest part of a wave form between two crests.

Weathering: The process by which rocks and minerals are broken down at or near Earth's surface.

Windward: On or toward the side facing into the wind.

Y

Yardang: Wind-sculpted, streamlined ridge that lies parallel to the prevailing winds.

Yazoo stream: A small stream that enters a floodplain and flows alongside a larger stream or river for quite a distance before eventually flowing into the larger waterway.

Z

Zooxanthellae: Microscopic algae that live symbiotically within the cells of some marine invertebrates, especially coral.

Fault

Earth's crust, the surface layer of the planet, is not solid and unbroken. The forces that rage inside the planet have fractured this brittle layer. Some of these fractures, called faults, lie beneath the surface of the crust. Other faults, however, have ruptured the surface, cracking the crust into various-sized blocks of rock. These blocks dip and rise along faults in response to pressure underground. One block may move up while the other moves down. Sometimes the movement is enough to form valleys or mountains. Other times that movement is not vertical but horizontal, as one block slips along the fault relative to the block on the other side.

Movement of crustal blocks along faults may be regular and slow or sporadic and sudden. When two blocks are forced to move against each other but are locked into position, stress builds up. When that stress becomes greater than the forces holding the blocks together, the blocks are forced to move suddenly and violently. The ground vibrations accompanying that release of energy are better known as an earthquake. There are more than one million earthquakes a year on Earth, though more than 60 percent of those are too faint to be felt. Crustal movements along faults are occurring continuously across most of the planet's surface.

The shape of the land

A fault is defined as a crack or fracture in Earth's crust along which rock on one side has moved relative to rock on the other. (When no movement has occurred, the fracture is known as a joint). When a fault breaks the planet's surface, it may range in length from a few inches to thousands of miles. The line on Earth's surface defining the fault is known as the fault line or fault trace.

Aerial view of the San Andreas Fault slicing through the Carrizo Plain just east of San Luis Obispo, California. The fault runs along most of the entire Pacific coast of California, extending for more than 800 miles.
PHOTOGRAPH REPRODUCED BY PERMISSION OF THE U.S. GEOLOGICAL SURVEY.

A fault may extend downward from the fault line at least several miles into the crust. The area where crustal blocks meet and move along a fault from the fault line down into the crust is known as the fault plane. The fault plane may be vertical in relation to Earth's surface. If so, the fault is known as a vertical fault. If the fault plane is slanted, the fault is known as an inclined fault. The crustal block that lies beneath the fault plane in an inclined fault is referred to as the footwall. The block that is above or seems to rest on the fault plane is referred to as the hanging wall. These terms do not apply if the fault plane is vertical.

Words to Know

Asthenosphere: The section of the mantle immediately beneath the lithosphere that is composed of partially melted rock.

Convection current: The circular movement of a gas or liquid between hot and cold areas.

Crust: The thin, solid outermost layer of Earth.

Dip: The measured angle from the horizontal plane (Earth's surface) to a fault plane or bed of rock.

Fault creep: The slow, continuous movement of crustal blocks along a fault.

Fault line: The line on Earth's surface defining a fault; also known as a fault trace.

Fault plane: The area where crustal blocks meet and move along a fault from the fault line down into the crust.

Fault scarp: A steep-sided ledge or cliff generated as a result of fault movement.

Fault system: A network of connected faults.

Footwall: The crustal block that lies beneath an inclined fault plane.

Graben: A block of Earth's crust dropped downward between faults.

Hanging wall: The crustal block that lies above an inclined fault plane.

Horst: A block of Earth's crust forced upward between faults.

Lithosphere: The rigid uppermost section of the mantle combined with the crust.

Mantle: The thick, dense layer of rock that lies beneath Earth's crust.

Plates: Large sections of Earth's lithosphere that are separated by deep fault zones.

Plate tectonics: The geologic theory that Earth's crust is composed of rigid plates that "float" toward or away from each other, either directly or indirectly, shifting continents, forming mountains and new ocean crust, and stimulating volcanic eruptions.

Strike: The compass direction of a fault line.

The measure of the angle between Earth's surface and the fault plane is called the fault's dip. Faults are classified according to how steeply they dip and the relative movement of the crustal blocks on either side of a fault. The movement of crustal blocks along a fault has been measured from 0.4 inch (1 centimeter) to 50 feet (15 meters). As mentioned, that movement may be slow or rapid. Slow, continuous movement is known as fault creep. Some faults creep from 0.5 inch (1.3 centimeters) to 4 inches (10 inches) a year.

Normal faults occur when underground pressure causes the crust to stretch or pull apart. When this happens, the hanging-wall block (the one above the fault plane) drops down relative to the footwall block. Most normal faults have dips of about 60 degrees. The resulting steep-sided ledge or cliff created at the top of the footwall block is called a fault scarp.

Normal faults usually occur in elevated regions such as plateaus. They are not often found singly in a landscape; typically, they occur in multiple arrangements, often in pairs of parallel faults. When movement

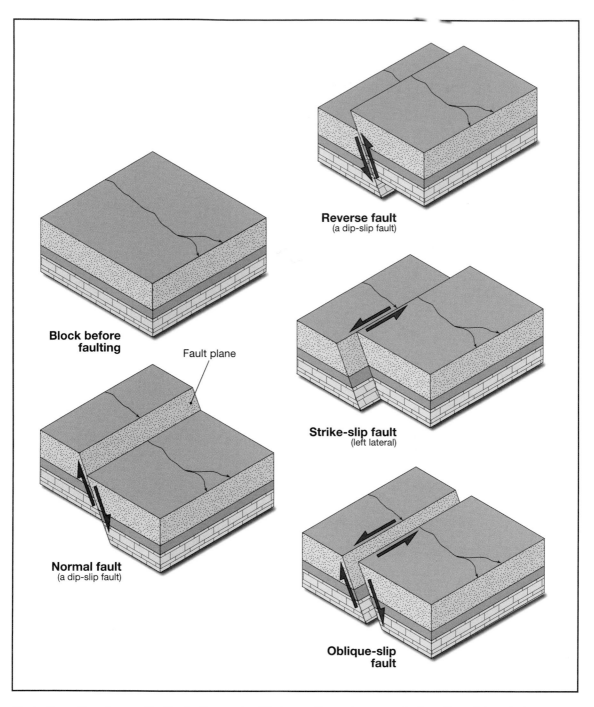

Illustration of four types of faults. Faults are classified according to how steeply they dip and the relative movement of the crustal blocks on either side of a fault. Normal faults, for example, occur when underground pressure causes the crust to stretch or pull apart, whereas reverse faults occur when underground pressure causes the crust to compress.

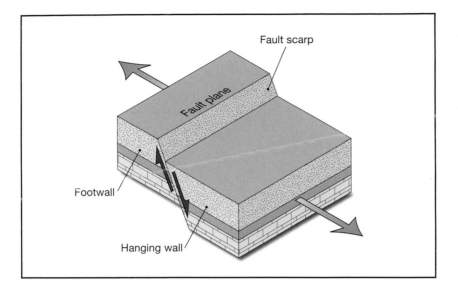

Fault scarp

Fault plane

Footwall

Hanging wall

When underground pressure causes the crust of normal faults to stretch or pull apart, the hanging-wall block drops down relative to the footwall block. The resulting steep-sided ledge or cliff created at the top of the footwall block is called a fault scarp.

takes place between parallel normal faults whose fault planes are angled downward toward each other (such as \ /), a crustal block may drop down between them. This down-dropped block, which forms a valley between the opposing footwall blocks, is called a graben (pronounced GRAH-bin). If the fault planes of the parallel faults are angled downward away from each other (such as / \), a crustal block between them may be elevated. This uplifted block is called a horst. A large horst that is lifted high can form a fault-block mountain. (For further information on fault-block mountains, see the **Mountain** chapter.) A series of uplifted and down-dropped blocks across a landscape is called a horst and graben structure. This feature is common in the western United States and northern Mexico.

In contrast, reverse faults occur when underground pressure causes the crust to compress, pushing blocks together. As two blocks are pushed together at a fault, the hanging-wall block is pushed up and over the foot-wall block. A fault scarp is created, but it takes the form of an overhanging ledge.

A special type of reverse fault is called a thrust fault (sometimes also called an overthrust fault). The fault plane of a thrust fault lies at a low angle to Earth's surface. This angle is less than 30 degrees. Because the angle is so low, the hanging-wall block is thrust up and over the footwall block. The movement is mainly horizontal as the hanging-wall block travels over the footwall block, sometimes for thousands of feet.

These previous faults are all categorized as dip-slip faults because the movement of the fault blocks is up or down along the fault plane. If the

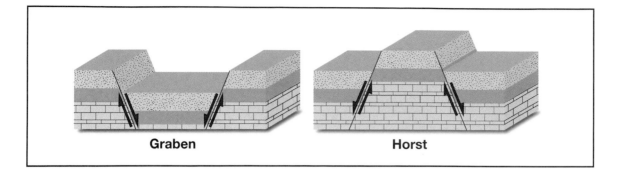

Graben   Horst

When fault planes are angled downward toward each other, a down-dropped block, called a graben, is formed. If the fault planes of the parallel faults are angled downward away from each other, a crustal block between them may be elevated. This uplifted block is called a horst.

movement is horizontal, with the two fault blocks scraping along side-by-side, the fault is known as a strike-slip fault (sometimes also known as a transcurrent or transverse fault). Strike is the compass direction—north, south, east, west—of the fault line or trace. The fault plane in a strike-slip fault is vertical or nearly vertical. There is little or no fault scarp created along this type of fault.

Strike-slip faults are classified according to the direction of motion of the blocks on either side of the fault. If the block on the opposite side of a strike-slip fault has moved to the left, it is a left-lateral strike-slip fault. If it has moved to the right, it is a right-lateral strike-slip fault. The relative motion, left or right, is the same regardless on which block an observer stands. The famous San Andreas Fault in California is a right-lateral strike-slip fault. Land west of the fault is edging northwest; land east is edging southeast.

In some faults, the movement is neither purely vertical nor horizontal, but a combination of the two. In instances where a fault has both normal and strike-slip movement or reverse and strike-slip movement, it is known as an oblique-slip fault. Although this type of fault is not unusual, it is far less common than normal, reverse, or strike-slip faults.

Forces and changes: Construction and destruction

Any rock subjected to intense stress or pressure over time will deform. At higher temperatures and pressures, rock will soften and bend. Geologists call this ductile deformation. At lower temperatures and pressures, however, rock will break or fracture instead of bending. This type of deformation, called brittle deformation, happens to rock in the upper part of Earth's crust. Faults are a clear example of brittle deformation.

The stress that is continually acting on and deforming Earth's surface may be in different forms: tensional stress, which stretches or pulls rock; compressional stress, which squeezes and squashes rock; and shear stress, which changes the shape of rock by causing adjacent parts to slide past

Blindly Faulting Los Angeles

In 1999, geologists mapped for the first time a major fault located directly beneath the city of Los Angeles, California. Named the Puente Hills Fault, it is a blind thrust fault, a type of thrust fault that does not break Earth's surface. This makes it difficult to identify. Comprised of three sections, it runs for nearly 25 miles (40 kilometers) under downtown Los Angeles, through Santa Fe Springs, and into the Coyote Hills of northern Orange County. The fault is approximately 12.5 miles (20 kilometers) wide. It is located about 2 miles (3.2 kilometers) beneath the surface in the center of Los Angeles, then dips to 10 miles (16 kilometers) underground as it continues northward. The entire fault system covers an area of roughly 250 square miles (650 square kilometers).

In the spring of 2003, geologists released a study reporting that the fault is capable of generating major earthquakes. They estimated that the fault has been responsible for some of the most severe earthquakes to strike southern California in the last 11,000 years. They also believed that the fault was responsible for the 1987 earthquake that hit near the city of Whittier, located about 12 miles (19 kilometers) from the center of downtown Los Angeles. Although a major earthquake along the fault will probably occur only once every 2,000 years, geologists believe many of the buildings in downtown Los Angeles will not be able to withstand such an earthquake when it comes.

one another. All of these stresses are directly related to events occurring deep within the planet. Earth's internal processes, from the core to the crust, have put the surface of the planet in motion, constantly changing its shape.

From the core to the crust

Geologists divide the surface and the interior of Earth into layers. At the very center of the planet is the core. It begins at a depth of about 1,800 miles (2,900 kilometers) beneath the surface and extends to a depth of 3,960 miles (6,370 kilometers). The core is composed of the metal elements iron and nickel, and it has a solid inner portion and a liquid outer portion. Temperatures in the core are estimated to exceed 9,900°F (5,482°C).

Above the core lies the thick mantle, which forms the main bulk of the planet's interior. Above the mantle lies the brittle crust, the thin shell of rock that covers Earth. The upper portion of the mantle is rigid. Geologists call the combination of this section of the mantle the overlying crust and the lithosphere (pronounced LITH-uh-sfeer). The lithosphere measures roughly 60 miles (100 kilometers) thick. The part of the mantle immediately beneath the lithosphere is called the asthenosphere (pronounced as-THEN-uh-sfeer). This layer is composed of partially melted rock that has the consistency of putty and extends to a depth of about 155 miles (250 kilometers).

The driving force in Earth's interior

The heat energy generated in the core is extreme. Earth's interior would melt if this energy were not released in some manner. Much like the circulating currents produced in a pot of boiling liquid on a hot stove, this energy is transported to the surface of the planet through currents called convection currents.

When a liquid in a pot begins to boil, it turns over and over. Liquid heated at the bottom of the pot rises to the surface because heating has caused it to expand and become less dense (lighter). Once at the surface, the heated liquid cools and becomes dense (heavier) once more. It then sinks back down to the bottom to become reheated. This continuous motion of heated material rising, cooling, and sinking forms the circular currents known as convection currents.

Similarly, when mantle rocks near the core are heated, they become less dense than the cooler, upper mantle rocks. These heated rocks then slowly rise through the mantle. When they reach the lithosphere, the heated rocks move along the base of the lithosphere, losing heat. Cooling and becoming denser, they then sink back toward the core, only to be heated once again. Scientists estimate that convection currents move mantle rock only an inch or two a year. It takes about 200 million years for heated rock to make a circular trip from the core to the lithosphere and back again.

Plate tectonics and faults

The slowly moving convection currents are able to release their heat energy near the surface of the planet because the lithosphere is broken into many pieces called tectonic or crustal plates. These plates, which vary in size and shape, "float" on the soft, semi-molten (melted) asthenosphere. As the convection currents move under the lithosphere, they exert dragging forces on the rigid tectonic plates above them. This causes the plates to move. Fitting together like pieces in a jigsaw puzzle, the plates are in constant contact with each other. Because they are interconnected, no single plate can move without affecting others. The movement or activity of one plate can influence another plate located thousands of miles away. The scientific theory explaining plates and their movements and interactions is called plate tectonics (a hypothesis is an educated guess; a theory is a principle supported by extensive scientific evidence and testing).

In general, tectonic plates inch their way across the surface of Earth at a rate no faster than human fingernails grow, roughly 2 inches (5 centimeters)

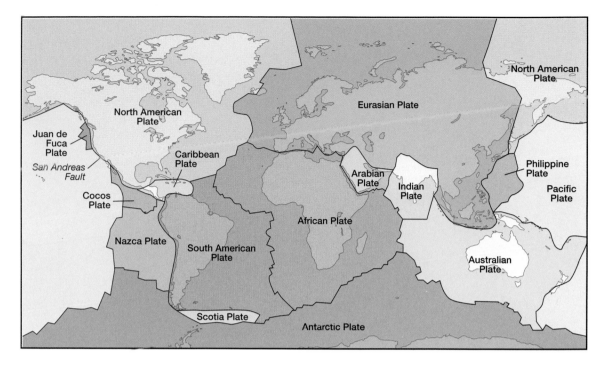

per year. As they move, the plates slide along each other (transform), move into each other (converge), or move away from each other (diverge). Plate margins are the boundaries or areas where the plates meet and interact.

The stresses that produce faulting are usually related to movements along plate margins. Although associated mainly with plate margins, faults can occur anywhere on Earth where the crust is weak. Normal faults are common in regions where the crust is being stretched and thinned as a result of plates diverging. Reverse faults are common in regions where the crust is being compressed and thickened as a result of plates converging. Thrust faults are even more common at convergent plate margins, where plates are moving toward one another, compressing, and often forming high mountains. Strike-slip faults are formed where unequal pressure causes rock sections to slip past each other. Major strike-slip faults occur between plates that are transforming. These special strike-slip plates are known as transform faults.

Earth's surface is broken into seven large and many small tectonic plates. These plates, each about 50 miles thick, move relative to one another an average of a few inches a year.

Spotlight on famous forms

Denali fault system, Alaska

Denali (pronounced de-NAHL-ee) is the name given by the Athabascan-speaking native people of Alaska to the mountain known as Mount McKinley, the highest mountain in North America at 20,320 feet

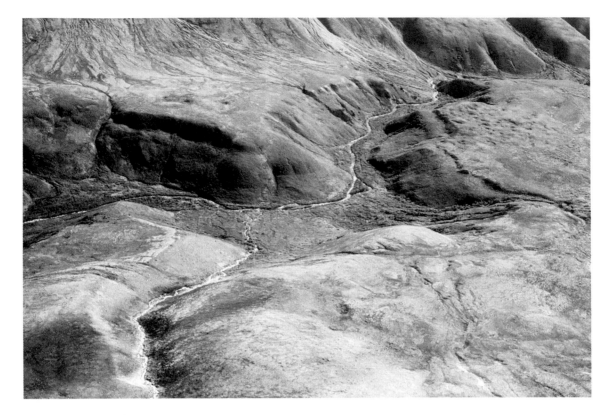

(6,194 meters). Translated, it means "the Great One." Denali is also the name of a great fault system (a network of connected faults) that extends for about 750 miles (1,200 kilometers) from southeast to southcentral Alaska. Predominantly composed of right-lateral strike-slip faults, Denali is one of the longest strike-slip fault systems in the world.

The Denali Fault marks the boundary where the Pacific Plate and the North American Plate meet and interact. Land south of the fault moves westward, and land north of the fault moves eastward. Geologists estimate that the two sides on the fault have slipped roughly 240 miles (386 kilometers) over the last 60 million years. On average, the plates move about 0.4 inch (1 centimeter) a year along the fault.

At times during the Denali Fault's history, the plates along it have locked up. Subsequent pressure builds up until it is finally released in an earthquake. This is what occurred on November 2, 2002, when an earthquake struck the fault about 90 miles (145 kilometers) south of Fairbanks, Alaska. One of the largest ever recorded in the United States, the earthquake measured 7.9 on the Richter scale (a scale developed by American seismologist Charles Richter to describe the amount of energy released by an earthquake). The earthquake ruptured 155 miles (260 kilometers) of the fault. Movement on the fault caused ground north of the fault to move eastward up to 26 feet (8 meters) relative to ground south of the fault.

New Madrid fault system, Central United States

The New Madrid fault system is a series of faults beneath the continental crust in the central United States. The system exists in the middle of the North American plate where tensional stress created a weak spot known as the Reelfoot rift. Called an intraplate fault system, it is a type of fault system that is still not clearly understood by geologists.

The faults along the system—normal, reverse, and strike-slip—lie 10 to 12 miles (16 to 19 kilometers) beneath Earth's surface. They create no fault lines. The New Madrid fault system extends at least 150 miles (240 kilometers) from Cairo, Illinois, to Marked Tree, Arkansas. It runs beneath the lines of five states: Illinois, Kentucky, Missouri, Tennessee, and Arkansas. It runs beneath the Mississippi River in three areas and the Ohio River in two areas. Movement along the system ranges from 1.5 to 2.8 inches (4 to 7 centimeters) a year.

More earthquakes occur in the area of the New Madrid fault system than in any other area of the United States east of the Rocky Mountains. More than 200 earthquakes are recorded on the system each year, but the vast majority of those cannot be felt. Only about 8 to 10 earthquakes a year are large enough to be felt (measuring 3.0 or more on the Richter scale).

In the winter of 1811–1812, three earthquakes centered on the New Madrid fault system were felt across the continent, from Canada to the Gulf of Mexico, and from the Rocky Mountains to the Atlantic coast. Present-day geologists estimate the largest of the earthquakes measured 8.8 on the Richter scale. The effects were widespread and severe. The most intense earthquake altered the course of the Mississippi River and created a depression in northwest Tennessee that filled with water to become Reelfoot Lake. Aftershocks (earthquake tremors that occur after the main shock) were felt around the region for a year afterward.

San Andreas Fault, California

The well-known San Andreas Fault in California is perhaps the most-studied fault in the world. It is the main fault in an intricate fault system; many smaller faults branch from and join the larger fault. The fault system is located along almost the entire Pacific coast of California, extending for more than 800 miles (1,287 kilometers). Its fault plane reaches down at least 10 miles (16 kilometers) into Earth's crust. Its fault line is a zone of crushed and broken rock that ranges from a few hundred feet to 1 mile (1.6 kilometers) wide.

A right-lateral strike-slip fault, the San Andreas Fault represents the boundary where the North American Plate and the Pacific Plate meet. Along the fault, the two plates scrape against each other as the North American Plate slips to the southeast and the Pacific Plate slips to the northwest. The rate of movement along the fault is about 0.8 to 1.4 inches (2 to 3.5 centimeters) a year. Because it is situated between plates that are transforming, the San Andreas Fault is also considered a transform fault.

Geologists believe the San Andreas Fault came into existence about 15 to 20 million years ago. They estimate that the total movement along the fault since that time has been at least 350 miles (563 kilometers). Thousands of earthquakes, most of which are too small to be felt, occur along the fault regularly. Over the last 1,500 years, large earthquakes along the fault have occurred every 150 years or so. The last recorded large earthquake on the southern portion of the fault took place in 1857. In 1906, a devastating earthquake occurred in the San Francisco region. The plates, which had been locked along the fault, ruptured and tore the ground apart along a 290-mile (467-kilometer) stretch. The ground west of the fault shifted northward as much as 21 feet (6.4 meters) in places.

For More Information

Books

Collier, Michael. *A Land in Motion: California's San Andreas Fault.* Berkeley, CA: University of California Press, 1999.

Harden, Deborah R. *California Geology.* Englewood Cliffs, NJ: Prentice Hall, 1997.

Knox, Ray, and David Stewart. *The New Madrid Fault Finders Guide.* Marble Hill, MO: Gutenberg-Richter Publications, 1995.

Web Sites

"Fault Motion." *Incorporated Research Institutions for Seismology.* http://www.iris.edu/gifs/animations/faults.htm (accessed on September 1, 2003).

"Faults." *Plate Tectonics.* http://www.platetectonics.com/book/page_15.asp (accessed on September 1, 2003).

"Hayward Fault." *The Berkeley Seismological Laboratory.* http://www.seismo.berkeley.edu/seismo/hayward/ (accessed on September 1, 2003).

Mustoe, M. *Every Place Has Its Faults!* http://www.tinynet.com/faults.html (accessed on September 1, 2003).

"The New Madrid Fault Zone." *The Arkansas Center for Earthquake Education and Technology Transfer.* http://quake.ualr.edu/public/nmfz.htm (accessed on May 5, 2003).

Schulz, Sandra S. and Robert E. Wallace. "The San Andreas Fault." *USGS.* http://pubs.usgs.gov/gip/earthq3/safaultgip.html (accessed on September 1, 2003).

Floodplain

Floodplains are landscapes shaped by running water. As streams and their larger forms, rivers, flow across the surface of land, they transport eroded rock and other material. (Erosion is the gradual wearing away of Earth surfaces through the action of wind and water.) At points along that journey, when their flow slows, the material they carry is dropped to create what are termed depositional landforms. Among these landforms are deltas and floodplains. (For further information on deltas, see the **Delta** chapter.)

The flooding of a stream or river is a natural and recurring event. Ancient cultures that lived along these waterways welcomed the flooding of the adjacent land. The material deposited enriched the soil, increasing its fertility for farming. For those along the Nile River in ancient Egypt, the annual flood was the "gift of the Nile." In many modern societies, however, the lands bordering rivers and streams are sites of homes, businesses, and other urban development. The flooding of this land is often a costly natural disaster.

The shape of the land

A floodplain (sometimes spelled flood plain) is an area of nearly flat land bordering a stream or river that is naturally subject to periodic flooding. A flood occurs when the flow of water in a stream becomes too high to be accommodated in the normal stream channel. The channel of a stream is the trench or depression filled with water as it flows across a landscape. The sides of the channel are known as the stream's banks. The bottom is the stream bed.

In a flood, water flows over the stream's banks, submerging the adjacent land. Depending on the amount of water, the flood may cover all or part of the floodplain. As water flows out of the stream's channel, it

A floodplain, like this one along the Limpopo River in southern Africa, is an area of nearly flat land bordering a stream or river that is naturally subject to periodic flooding. **PHOTOGRAPH REPRODUCED BY PERMISSION OF THE CORBIS CORPORATION.**

immediately slows down. The material carried by the stream—sediment such as gravel, sand, silt, and clay—is deposited on the floodplain. Large particles are deposited first, and much of this material is laid down alongside both banks. This process, repeated over and over, forms low ridges or mounds known as natural levees (pronounced LEH-veez). Levees built by humans along rivers in an effort to control flooding are known as artificial levees. Natural levees are composed primarily of gravel and sand. They are steep on the side facing the stream channel and gently sloping on the other side. Varying greatly in size, levees may be several feet in height and up to a mile or more in width.

The finer sediments transported by the floodwater, silt and clay, are deposited on the floor of the floodplain away from the levees. The general term for sediment deposited by running water is alluvium (pronounced ah-LOO-vee-em). Because floodplains are covered with alluvium, they are often called alluvial plains. Lower, poorly drained areas on the floodplain that not only collect alluvium but also retain water are known as backswamps.

Floodplains are widened as a stream snakes its way across a landscape. Streams and rivers rarely flow in straight lines. They have a natural tendency to flow along a path of least resistance, eroding any soft material along their banks. Because of this, many stream channels form a series of smooth bends or curves called meanders (pronounced me-AN-ders). The term comes from the Menderes River in southwest Turkey, which is noted for its snakelike or winding course. As a stream begins to meander, erosion will take place on the outer parts of the bends or curves where the velocity or speed of water is highest. These eroded areas are called cut banks. Sediment will be deposited along the inner bends where the velocity is lowest. These deposits are known as point bars. As erosion and deposition continues, a stream tends to change shape and shift position across its floodplain, which enlarges in response to the stream's back-and-forth movement.

Eventually, a meander forms a tighter and tighter curve until it almost becomes a complete loop. The stream then shortens its course by eroding through the intervening land or neck of the loop, especially during times of flooding. Sediment is deposited, isolating the meander from the stream. Still filled with water, the crescent-shaped meander is called an oxbow lake (because it resembles the U-shaped collar used with teams of oxen). In Australia, an oxbow lake is known as billabong (pronounced bill-ah-BONG); in Louisiana and Mississippi, it is sometimes called a bayou (pronounced BY-oo). Over time, as the floodplain is repeatedly submerged under water, alluvium fills an oxbow lake, turning it into a marsh and eventually into a meander scar. The dry meander scar, which typically only holds water during rains, still retains the shape of the original meander.

Words to Know

Alluvium: A general term for sediment (rock debris such as gravel, sand, silt, and clay) deposited by running water.

Backswamp: The lower, poorly drained area of a floodplain that retains water.

Erosion: The gradual wearing away of Earth surfaces through the action of wind and water.

Levee (natural): A low ridge or mound along a stream bank, formed by deposits left when floodwater slows down on leaving the channel.

Meander: A bend or loop in a stream's course.

Oxbow lake: A crescent-shaped body of water formed from a single loop that was cut off from a meandering stream.

Silt: Fine earthy particles that are smaller than sand and carried by moving water and deposited as a sediment.

Terrace: The exposed portion of a former floodplain that stands like a flat bench above the outer edges of the new floodplain.

Yazoo stream: A small stream that enters a floodplain and flows alongside a larger stream or river for quite a distance before eventually flowing into the larger waterway.

A small stream that enters a floodplain and flows alongside a larger stream or river for quite a distance is known as a yazoo stream or yazoo tributary. It helps drain the floodplain, but is often prevented from joining the main stream by the stream's natural levee. Only when it finds a low or weak place in the levee does it flow naturally into the larger stream. The term describing this type of small stream comes from the Yazoo River, which flows parallel to the Mississippi River for 175 miles (282 kilometers) before it joins with the larger river.

Over long periods of time, a stream or river may erode its bed down to a lower level, putting its old floodplain out of reach of flooding. A new floodplain then forms with the old floodplain standing above its outer edges in the form of a flat bench. This exposed portion of the former floodplain is known as a terrace. (For more information, see the **Stream and river** chapter.)

Forces and changes: Construction and destruction

Running water is the primary force of erosion on the planet. Streams and major rivers are continuously at work moving rock fragments and dissolved materials from elevated landmasses to oceans, lakes, and other streams and rivers. Worldwide, streams transport 16 billion tons (14.5 billion metric tons) of sediment per year. They alter landscapes through both erosion and deposition.

Life of a stream

Geologists characterize streams as youthful, mature, and old. When a stream is in its youthful stage, it has a fairly straight channel and a steep gradient (the slope it runs down). It generally flows in a V-shaped valley in a highland or mountainous area. Its velocity is high, and it is actively lowering its channel through erosion in order to reach base level. This refers to the point at which the stream or river reaches the elevation of the large body of water, such a lake or ocean, into which it drains. While aided by gravity, a stream will downcut or erode its channel deeper and deeper in order to reach the level of its final destination as quickly as possible. If the difference in height between the stream or river and its destination is great, so will be the erosive or cutting force of the stream. In this stage, a stream has little, if any, floodplain.

By the time a stream reaches its mature stage, its gradient and velocity are moderate. The valley it flows through is more U-shaped with rounded hills. Because it has slowed down, the stream begins to meander. While it is still eroding downward, the stream's main force of erosion is lateral (horizontal) as it begins winding back and forth, carving out a valley floor between valley walls or bluffs. Periodically, the stream will flood all or a part of its valley, depositing alluvium on its developing floodplain.

An old age stream has reached its base level, and its gradient and velocity are very low. It has lost its ability to erode downward. In fact, it deposits as much material as it erodes. The stream meanders greatly in its nearly flat valley. It has an extensive, well-developed floodplain marked with oxbow lakes.

Moving material

Streams and rivers are conduits for transporting sediment. The ability of a stream to move sediment depends on the velocity of water in the stream and the size of the sediment particles. Water moving at a low velocity can move only small, fine particles such as sand, silt, and clay. Sand is a mineral particle with a diameter between 0.002 and 0.08 inch (0.005 and 0.2 centimeter); silt is a mineral particle with a diameter between 0.00008 and 0.002 inch (0.0002 and 0.005 centimeter); clay is a mineral particle with a diameter less than 0.00008 inch (0.0002 centimeter). Water moving at a high velocity can move both small particles and large, coarse particles such as boulders.

A stream will continue to carry its load of sediment as long as its velocity remains constant or increases (if it increases, it can carry an even larger load). Any change in the geography of the landscape that causes a stream channel to bend or rise will slow the flow of water in a stream. As soon as a stream's speed decreases, it loses the ability to carry all of its load and a portion will be deposited, depending on how much the stream slows down. Particles will be deposited by size with the largest settling out first.

What Is a 100-year Flood?

Large floods are often given designations that describe the statistical probability or chance when they might occur. A flood can be termed a 10-, 20-, 50-, 100-, or 500-year flood based on its expected recurrence. The larger the flood, the larger the "year." A 100-year flood, for example, is determined to be the maximum amount of flood to be expected in a 100-year period. A 20-year flood is the maximum amount of flood to be expected in a 20-year period.

This does not mean, however, that a 100-year flood will strike only once every one hundred years. It means that there is a one in one hundred, or 1 percent, chance of a flood of such magnitude occurring in any given year. Depending on rain and other weather conditions, a 100-year flood may be followed by another similar flood only a month, a year, or twenty years later.

In March 1973, as a result of rain and snow melt, a 100-year flood occurred on the Mississippi River. Just twenty years later, the Mississippi River was subjected to an even larger flood. One of the largest floods in U.S. history, it affected some 16,000 square miles (41,000 square kilometers) and caused property damage in excess of $15 billion. Forty-eight people died in the severe flooding.

Floods

Floods occur when excessive rainfall or melting snow produces more water than the soil can absorb and a stream can normally carry in its channel. Several things happen to a stream when it floods. The increase in the amount of water causes the stream to flow much more rapidly than usual. This, in turn, greatly increases the amount and size of the sediment the stream can transport. Large boulders in stream beds are moved during floods.

When a stream overflows its banks, its floodplain increases the area of the stream's channel. Flowing in this now much-wider channel, the water immediately loses velocity, and its load of sediment is deposited. As is always the case, larger particles drop out first, forming levees alongside the stream. The finer-grained silts and clays are carried farther out onto the floodplain where they settle after the waters of the flood recede.

A floodplain becomes flooded on average once every year or two, most often during the season with the highest amount of rainfall. As the flooding process occurs over and over, meander curves enlarge, alluvium is constantly reworked, and the floodplain widens. The continual wetting and drying causes the sediment to be compacted in the levees. The highest points on a floodplain, natural levees may grow large enough to control the amount of flooding that occurs.

Sought-after land

Silt and clay deposited on a floodplain make the soil there extremely fertile. As a result, a floodplain is rich agricultural land. The disadvantage of farming on a floodplain is the natural hazard of floods. Ancient civilizations were aware of the recurring nature of floods on streams and rivers, and they planned their plantings accordingly. In the present day, rivers are important sources of water, power, and transportation. Fertile floodplains are sites of increasing urban development.

To control small annual floods that threaten homes and businesses, many communities have erected artificial levees. These walls built along a river to prevent high water from leaving the channel seem to work well for small floods. However, the levees upset the natural function of a floodplain, which acts as a reservoir for the excess water. Instead, the flood moves downstream until it finds a place not protected by artificial levees. And no artificial levee can be constructed high enough to contain very large, unpredictable floods.

The building of dams is another method used to control flooding, and these structures work to a degree. They store water in artificial reservoirs that can be used during dry seasons or at other times when water levels are

The Tonle Sap Great Lake in Cambodia is the largest freshwater lake in Southeast Asia. Every year the waters of the Mekong River flood into the lake to inundate some 1.25 million hectares of land for a period of several months. Cambodian culture has adapted to and flourished with the annual flooding, and life there is closely connected with the rise and fall of the waters.
PHOTOGRAPH REPRODUCED BY PERMISSION OF THE CORBIS CORPORATION.

low. The release of that stored water in a controlled manner can also help generate electricity.

Like artificial levees, however, dams may be overwhelmed by large floods, leading to disaster for those living downstream of the dam. Dams also trap sediment, so land downstream is deprived of material that would make it fertile. The natural conditions on a floodplain are destroyed, and farmers must turn to chemical fertilizers and other artificial means to help crops grow. This increases both economic and environmental cost. Over the course of perhaps a few hundred years, the sediment trapped by a dam will eventually fill its reservoir, and the dam will become useless.

Spotlight on famous forms

Mississippi River floodplain, United States

The Mississippi River is one of the world's great rivers in terms of both the amount of water it carries and its length. It flows south across the United States, somewhere east of the country's center, and empties into the Gulf of Mexico in a great delta. It runs for about 2,350 miles (3,780 kilometers). It has many tributaries, the most important of which are the Arkansas, Ohio, and Missouri Rivers.

The Mississippi River is divided into two main sections: the upper Mississippi runs from its source in Minnesota to the city of Thebes in southern Illinois where it meets the Ohio River, and the lower Mississippi runs from this point south to the Gulf of Mexico. The river's floodplain encompasses more than 30 million acres (12 million hectares). Most of this floodplain, approximately 25 million acres (10 million hectares), occurs adjacent to the lower Mississippi, which meanders in great loops. Natural levees, oxbow lakes, and marshes mark this area.

The Mississippi River is one of the most heavily engineered natural features in the United States. The character of its floodplain has changed to accommodate agriculture and urban development. Ninety percent of the floodplain lies behind levees, many of which have been artificially created. Twenty-eight locks and dams were constructed on the upper Mississippi River to allow the passage of ships. As a result, much of the river's floodplain fails to receive its revitalizing seasonal floods. Extensive water pollution has also affected the river and its floodplain.

Nile River floodplain, Egypt

The Nile River is the longest river in the world. It runs approximately 4,160 miles (6,695 kilometers) from the Luvironza River in Burundi in central Africa to the Mediterranean Sea on the northeast coast of Egypt.

It flows toward the Mediterranean, draining about 1,100,000 square miles (2,850,000 square kilometers) of land, which is about one-tenth of the area of the African continent.

In ancient times, the Nile River flooded annually, caused by rains in central Africa and melting snow and rains in the Ethiopian highlands. The river was at its lowest point in May, but from June to August it rose rapidly, carrying great quantities of silt in its waters that flowed out over the river's floodplain. The flood was at its highest point in mid-September. By October the waters began to recede, leaving pools of water in back-swamps. After the water was absorbed by the soil, the ancient Egyptians planted their crops in the fertile floodplain.

In 1970 the Egyptian government completed construction of the Aswan High Dam on the Nile just south of the city of Aswan, ending the annual floods on the river. The dam, which formed the artificial Lake Nasser behind it, helps provide hydroelectric power and water for irrigation projects. It has also prevented silt from being carried further downstream, trapping 98 percent of the river's rich sediments. Since then, farmers along the Nile have been forced to use large amounts of chemical fertilizers, which have washed into the river, contaminating it and other

Part of the upper Mississippi River cutting through sandstone. The river's floodplain encompasses more than 30 million acres and mostly occurs adjacent to the lower Mississippi.
PHOTOGRAPH REPRODUCED BY PERMISSION OF THE CORBIS CORPORATION.

The Pantanal, which covers more than 77,000 square miles in Brazil, is considered one of Earth's richest ecosystems. It is a landscape of swamps, seasonally flooded grasslands and woodlands, and different types of forest.
PHOTOGRAPH REPRODUCED BY PERMISSION OF THE CORBIS CORPORATION.

water sources. Because the river does not bring new sediment to areas downstream, soil erosion has become an additional problem.

Pantanal, Brazil

The Pantanal (pronounced pen-te–NAL; Portuguese for "swamp") is a land area covering approximately 77,220 square miles (200,000 square kilometers). Lying mostly in west-central Brazil, the Pantanal also reaches into eastern Bolivia and northeastern Paraguay. During the wet season, from November to April, this vast floodplain of the Paraguay River and its tributaries becomes partially submerged. Average annual rainfall in this area measures between 39 and 55 inches (100 and 140 centimeters).

The slope of the land is very slight, and the rivers and streams cannot carry the excess amount of water. The floodplain is swamped by a flood that takes six months to travel the length of the Pantanal from north to south. Areas of the floodplain are alternately flooded, then left dry with only a few spots of water remaining.

The Pantanal is considered one of Earth's richest ecosystems (an ecosystem is a system formed by the interaction of a community of plants, animals, and microorganisms with their environment). It is a landscape of swamps, seasonally flooded grasslands and woodlands, and different types of forest. This mixture helps the Pantanal house the highest concentration of wildlife in both North and South America. Approximately 700 species of birds inhabit the area. It is also one of the last refuges for many threatened South American mammals, including jaguars, pumas, manned wolves, giant otters, giant anteaters, giant armadillos, and marsh deer

For More Information

Books

Bridge, John S. *Rivers and Floodplains: Forms, Processes, and Sedimentary Record.* Malden, MA: Blackwell, 2002.

Web Sites

"Basics of Flooding." *Floodplain Management Association.* http://www.floodplain.org/flood_basics.htm (accessed on September 1, 2003).

"Floodplain Features and Management." *Shippensburg University.* http://www.ship.edu/~cjwolt/geology/fpl.htm (accessed on September 1, 2003).

"Floods and Flood Plains." *U.S. Geological Survey.* http://water.usgs.gov/pubs/of/ofr93-641/ (accessed on September 1, 2003).

Geyser and hot spring

An eponym (pronounced EH-puh-nim) is something or someone that gives its name to everything of its type. In geology, two general landforms derive their names from those of specific examples. Vulcano is the name of an island in the Tyrrhenian Sea north of Sicily. Every volcano on the planet owes its name to this small volcanic island. Geysir (Icelandic for "gusher") is the name of an erupting flow of heated water from the ground in Iceland. The name, in the form geyser, is applied to all such landforms that eject a column of hot water.

Volcano and geyser share more than the fact they derive from eponyms. Both arise as the result of volcanic activity. Whereas volcanoes spew lava (called magma when it is beneath Earth's surface), geysers emit hot water and steam. The activity of geysers is labeled hydrothermal (from the Greek words *hydro,* meaning "water," and *therme,* meaning "heat"). Hydrothermal activity also creates hot springs, fumaroles, and mud pots. Some of these landforms emit small-scale eruptions; all are beautiful and delicate.

The shape of the land

A geyser is considered a type of hot spring, which is a pool of hot water that has seeped through a vent or opening in Earth's surface. By definition, the temperature of the water is at least 15°F (8.3°C) warmer than the average temperature of the surrounding air. It can reach as high as 200°F (93°C). Normal hot springs do not erupt, but may seem to churn and "boil" as gases from underground pass through them. When the water that feeds a hot spring passes through rocks underground, it may dissolve minerals from the rocks and bring them to the surface. If those rocks are volcanic, then the water carries silica to the surface. (Silica is the most abundant element found in magma.) At the surface, the water cools and

the silica forms geyserite (pronounced GUY-zuh-rite), a white or grayish cauliflowerlike deposit that creates rims or terraces around the spring. This deposit is also known as sinter. If the water passes through limestone, then it carries calcium carbonate to the surface. There the mineral crystallizes to form travertine (pronounced TRA-ver-teen). This dense, white rock also creates ledges and other rock formations around the spring. The water and rocks in hot springs may be multicolored. Brilliant rings of red, blue, brown, green, orange, and yellow are formed by the different species of algae and bacteria that flourish in the hot spring environment.

A geyser is a hot spring that periodically erupts through an opening in Earth's surface, spewing hot water and steam up to hundreds of feet above the ground. Essential geological conditions must be met for a geyser to exist: among other conditions, it must have an abundant water supply, an intense heat source, and a special plumbing system. Because of this, geysers are rare. There are only approximately seven hundred geysers known to exist on Earth. Yellowstone National Park, which lies in northwest Wyoming and extends into Montana and Idaho, contains more than four hundred geysers. The two types of geysers are fountain geysers and cone geysers. As their name implies, fountain geysers erupt like a fountain in various directions through a pool that fills an open crater before or during the eruption. After the eruption, the pool may drain completely into the geyser's vent. Cone geysers erupt in a fairly narrow jet from a vent in a conelike mound formed of geyserite.

A fumarole (pronounced FYOO-ma-role) is a small hole or vent in Earth's surface through which volcanic gases escape from underground. Fumaroles are also known as steam vents because the most common gas they emit is water vapor or steam. These types of hot springs have little water in their system. What does enter the system is boiled away before it reaches the surface. This leaves only steam and small amounts of foul-smelling gases such as hydrogen sulfide (the aroma of rotten eggs) and sulfur dioxide (the initial biting aroma of a lit match). Sometimes as the sulfur dioxide cools when it escapes from the vent, the sulfur in the vapor crystallizes around the vent, forming yellow deposits. The temperature of the gases emitted from a fumarole may reach as high as 750°F (400°C).

A mud pot (sometimes spelled mudpot) is a type of hot spring that contains thick muddy clay. Although mud pots have slightly more water than fumaroles, they also contain the volcanic gases present in the steam vents. In particular, they contain hydrogen sulfide. When this gas

---

OPPOSITE The Pohutu Geyser, New Zealand, rises up to 59 feet and is the most significant in a major geyser field of more than five hundred hot springs and other forms of geothermal activity. **PHOTOGRAPH REPRODUCED BY PERMISSION OF PHOTO RESEARCHERS, INC.**

Words to Know

Crust: The thin, solid outermost layer of Earth.

Fumarole: A small hole or vent in Earth's surface through which volcanic gases escape from underground.

Geyser: A hot spring that periodically erupts through an opening in Earth's surface, spewing hot water and steam.

Geyserite: A white or grayish silica-based deposit formed around hot springs.

Groundwater: Freshwater lying within the uppermost parts of Earth's crust.

Hot spring: A pool of hot water that has seeped through an opening in Earth's surface.

Lithosphere: The rigid uppermost section of the mantle combined with the crust.

Mantle: The thick, dense layer of rock that lies beneath Earth's crust.

Mud pot: A hot spring that contains thick, muddy clay.

Plates: Large sections of Earth's lithosphere that are separated by deep fault zones.

Plate tectonics: The geologic theory that Earth's crust is composed of rigid plates that "float" toward or away from each other, either directly or indirectly, shifting continents, forming mountains and new ocean crust, and stimulating volcanic eruptions.

Rhyolite: A fine-grained type of volcanic rock that has a high silica content.

Travertine: A dense, white deposit formed from calcium carbonate that creates rock formations around hot springs.

combines with water, it forms sulfuric acid. At a mud pot's surface, the acid dissolves the surrounding surface rock, thickening the water with muddy clay. Steam and other gases bubble up through the layers of mud, often explosively so. Mud pots are usually gray or light brownish-gray in color. Sometimes, minerals from the dissolved rocks tint the mud with shades of pink, red, and other colors. When this occurs, the mud pot is also called a paint pot.

Forces and changes: Construction and destruction

Hydrothermal activity occurs around the world, but it is most abundant (and spectacular) in Iceland, the North Island of New Zealand, and in Yellowstone National Park. In these areas, water underground comes in contact with heated rocks and magma, then travels up to the planet's surface through a maze of cracks and fractures, an underground plumbing system. Without this water and this heat, and a way for their creation to reach the surface, these boiling, bubbling, hissing, spewing, spouting, and gushing landforms would never exist.

Water under the surface

The thin, rocky outer layer that forms Earth's surface is the crust. Lying within it is a layer of freshwater of varying thickness that fills the pore spaces

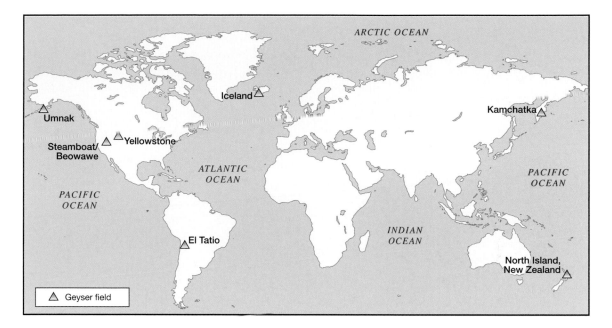

and microscopic openings in rocks and sediment. These openings include the spaces between grains of sand as well as cracks and fractures in rocks. As rain or melted snow seeps through the ground, some of it clings to particles of soil or to roots of plants. Water not used by plants moves ever deeper into the crust, drawn downward by gravity, until it reaches a layer of rock or sediment through which it cannot easily pass. It then fills the empty spaces and cracks above that layer. This water is known as groundwater. The volume of groundwater held in Earth's crust is forty times greater than all the freshwater in the planet's lakes and streams.

The area where groundwater fills all the spaces and pores underground is called the zone of saturation. The top surface of this zone is called the water table. Above it, the pores and spaces in rock hold mainly air, along with some water. This is called the zone of aeration. In places where rainfall is plentiful, the zone of aeration is usually less than 100 feet (30 meters) thick. In certain areas, such as at a pond's edge, the zone of saturation comes to the surface and the zone of aeration has essentially no thickness. In other areas, such as under some deserts, the zone of aeration may extend down from the surface for hundreds of feet before the water table is reached.

Location of the major geyser fields around the world. Hydrothermal activity occurs around the world, but it is most abundant in Iceland, the North Island of New Zealand, and in Yellowstone National Park.

Earth's heated interior

On average, the temperature of the crust increases with increasing depth. The temperature of the first 10 to 15 feet (3 to 5 meters) or so of the crust below the surface is the same as the average annual temperature of the external air. Below that, the temperature increases roughly 4.5°F every 330 feet (2.5°C every 100 meters). In the mantle, the thick layer of rock lying beneath the crust, the temperature continues to rise, though not at the same rate. It may do so slowly, or it may do so quickly, perhaps at a rate more than ten times that in the crust. In the core at the center of the planet, temperatures are believed to exceed 9,900°F (5,482°C).

If the heat energy generated by the extreme temperatures at Earth's core were not released in some manner, the interior of the planet would melt. This energy is carried to the surface of the planet by convection currents, the circular movement of molten material deep within Earth. What occurs is similar to what takes place in a pot of boiling water or other liquid. When a liquid in a pot begins to boil, it turns over and over. Liquid heated at the bottom of the pot rises to the surface because heating has caused it to expand and become less dense (lighter). Once at the surface, the heated material cools and becomes denser (heavier) once more. It then sinks back down to the bottom to become reheated. This continuous motion of heated material rising, cooling, and sinking forms the circular-moving convection currents.

Near the core, mantle rocks are heated, becoming less dense and lighter than the surrounding material. They then rise toward the rigid lithosphere (pronounced LITH-uh-sfeer; the upper section of the mantle combined with the overlying crust) at a rate of about a few inches per year. While this occurs, colder, denser, and heavier rocks near base of the lithosphere tend to sink. Near the core, they become heated and rise to the surface once again, and the cycle continues.

The pressure created by the movement of the convection currents under the lithosphere has broken that rigid layer into sections that move about the planet's surface in response to the moving currents. Geologists call these sections plates. The scientific theory explaining how and why the plates move is known as plate tectonics. The movement of the plates—into one another, away from one another, or under one another—has directly or indirectly created (and continues to create) many of the geologic features on the surface of Earth.

Hydrothermal activity: Water and heat

Hydrothermal landforms—hot springs, geysers, fumaroles, and mud pots—are primarily found above areas in the crust where magma or molten rock has risen to a shallow depth beneath the surface. In such instances, the magma may exist in a chamber or reservoir 3 to 6 miles (5 to 10 kilometers) beneath Earth's surface. This magma may be part of heated rock from a convection current or may be part of the leading edge of a plate that has moved under another plate. Geologists called this type

Ancient Water

The total amount of water that exists on the planet—in the oceans, lakes, rivers, ice caps, groundwater and atmosphere—is a fixed quantity. That amount is about 500 quintillion gallons (1,900 quintillion liters). Scientists believe this amount has not changed in the last three billion years. The water that existed then exists now.

Scientists estimate the amount of time for groundwater to circulate downward, become heated, and reappear on the surface of the planet in the form of a geyser is about 500 years. The water spouting from geysers in the present day fell to the surface of Earth as rain or snow at about the time Europeans discovered North America. The water gushing from the hot springs in Hot Springs National Park in Arkansas is even older: scientists have determined that this water is over 4,000 years old.

of plate movement subduction. It occurs when an oceanic plate moves into another oceanic plate or into a continental (land) plate. Because the oceanic plate is dense, it slides under the other plate. As it travels downward into the mantle, high temperature and pressure melt the rock at the leading edge of the plate, forming thick, flowing magma. Since it is less dense than the rock that typically surrounds it deep underground, magma tends to rise toward Earth's surface. Driven by pressure created by gas bubbles within it, the magma forces its way through weakened layers of rock to collect in magma chambers. Sometimes pressure builds up within the chamber, forcing the magma through cracks or vents onto the surface of the planet. The vents through which the magma passes are known as volcanoes. (For more information on volcanoes, see the **Volcano** chapter.)

In fact, most hot springs, geysers, fumaroles, and mud pots are found in regions where volcanic activity is very young or has become inactive. In both cases, hot magma does not erupt onto the surface of the planet but exists to heat groundwater that enters the region above it. For example, geologists believe an incredible volcanic explosion 600,000 years ago left a partially molten magma chamber beneath the central portion of present-day Yellowstone National Park. It continues to supply the heat that helps create the many and varied hydrothermal landforms that mark the park. Geologists estimate that rocks in old magma chambers may remain hot for one million years or more.

In rare cases, hot springs may exist in areas where magma does not lie close to Earth's surface. Cracks in the crust and mantle may allow groundwater to seep thousands of feet underground. The natural heat of the surrounding rocks, ever increasing at greater depths, heats the water before it makes its way back to the surface.

The underground plumb-ing system of hot springs, fumaroles, mud pots, and geysers.

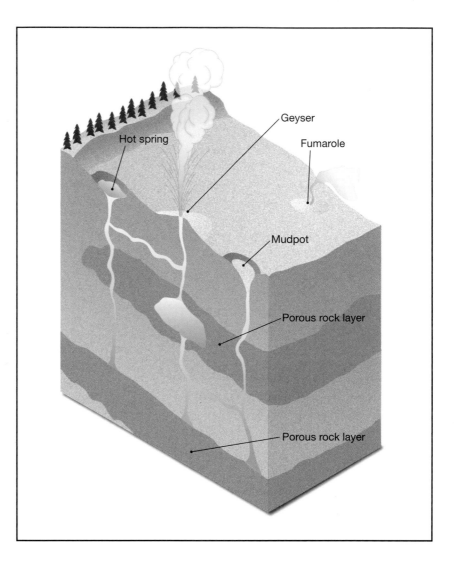

Plumbing systems

Hot springs, fumaroles, mud pots, and geysers all require some type of "plumbing system" to bring water, steam, and gases from several thousand feet underground to the surface. This underground system of cracks and fissures may be relatively open, allowing hot water to bubble slowly and continuously to the surface. Or the system may be restricted, keeping hot water and stream under pressure until it finally spews from the surface.

Hot springs form when there is an abundant supply of groundwater that collects in some sort of reservoir or cavity above heated rock or magma. The water is heated to temperatures exceeding 400°F (205°C). Even though water normally boils and begins to turn into steam at 212°F (100°C), this

superheated water remains in a liquid state because it is under intense pressure caused by the overlying rock and other groundwater. As the water becomes heated, it also becomes less dense than the cooler groundwater sinking in around it. Convection currents, much like in the mantle, are created that begin to carry the lighter, superheated water to the surface.

As it makes its way upward through its plumbing system, the hot water is able to dissolve minerals from the rocks lining the system. Most often, those rocks are rhyolite (pronounced RIE-uh-lite), a fine-grained type of volcanic rock that has a high silica content. Some of the dissolved silica forms geyserite that lines the walls of the plumbing system (the rest is carried to the surface where it forms geyserite there). This helps seal the system, preventing water from escaping into the surrounding rock. The closer the water is to the surface, the lower the pressure exerted on it. When it finally reaches the surface, the hot water does not burst forth, but merely fills the hot spring pool.

Steam rising from a thermal pool in Yellowstone National Park, Wyoming. The park contains the greatest number of geysers in the world.
PHOTOGRAPH REPRODUCED BY PERMISSION OF THE CORBIS CORPORATION.

Oldest Geyser

Located in the Upper Geyser Basin area of Yellowstone National Park is perhaps the world's oldest active geyser. Castle Geyser is a cone geyser that erupts every 9 to 11 hours. For the first 20 minutes of its eruption, the geyser shoots out a jet of water to heights between 60 and 90 feet (18 and 27 meters). For the following 40 minutes, it releases a column of noisy steam. The geyser is dramatic even when not erupting. Its geyserite cone stands 12 feet (3.7 meters) high, surrounded by terraces formed of travertine.

Geologists estimate that it has taken 5,000 to 15,000 years for Castle Geyser's cone to reach that height. What is remarkable is that the cone sits on top of an even more massive geyserite formation deposited by an earlier spring. Since geologists believe hot spring activity has been taking place at Yellowstone for at least 200,000 years, it is possible that this underlying formation is that old.

Fumaroles and mud pots differ from hot springs in the amount of water they hold in their plumbing systems. Fumaroles contain the least amount of water. The small amount of water that does collect underground above magma or heated rocks is boiled and converted to steam. The steam combines with gases released by the underground magma and rushes upward, creating a hissing or roaring sound as it escapes the opening at the surface. Mud pots, on the other hand, contain more water than fumaroles, though far less than hot springs. Only some of the water may be converted to steam. The rest rises to the surface in a heated state along with volcanic gases. At the surface, there is not enough water to wash away the sticky clay and mud formed when sulfuric acid dissolves the surrounding rock.

Geysers have the most complex plumbing system. Like hot springs, they have a reservoir that fills with groundwater deep underground. The water is heated by magma or hot rocks, but does not turn to steam because it is under pressure. Unlike hot springs, the water in geysers does not flow freely to the surface. Along a geyser's plumbing system, there are constrictions or bends that block that flow. Unable to flow upward, the water at the bottom is heated even more. Still, it does not completely vaporize because of the weight of the water above it. The steam that is created does flow upward in bubbles, collecting in the system's tight areas when they become too large or numerous to pass through. At a certain critical point, the bubbles then lift the water above, forcing some of it out of the geyser at the surface. This allows the pressure in the system to decrease. With a sudden drop in pressure, much of the superheated water in the system turns quickly into steam, which expands to over 1,500 times its original,

liquid volume. This tremendous expansion forces the water out of the geyser in an eruption. As the eruption continues, the heat and pressure in the system decrease. When the water in the reservoir is depleted, the eruption stops. Groundwater then begins to refill the reservoir, and the cycle begins again.

Temporary features

Providing the groundwater supply is constant, geysers erupt at regular intervals. However, geysers are often temporary features geologically. They do not last for millions of years. They may only last for a few thousand. Along with hot springs, fumaroles, and mud pots, geysers are natural features whose structure may be easily disturbed by changes in the crust. Earthquakes and tremors may shift the ground, changing the flow of groundwater or altering the plumbing system. And, unfortunately, the beauty of these landforms may bring about their destruction. Eager to see an eruption of any type, people have thrown material into the vents and pools. Coins, logs, rocks, blankets, laundry: the list of material is endless. Instead of coaxing an eruption, this has often disturbed the delicate condition under which these landforms exist.

Spotlight on famous forms

Great Geysir, Iceland

The geyser that gave its name to all others lies in a valley named Haukadalur in southern Iceland. A volcanic island (marked by more than two hundred volcanoes), Iceland boasts more hot springs and other hydrothermal activity than any other country. Of the almost eight hundred hot springs on the island, the most famous is the Great Geysir. Geologists estimate that it was created at the end of the thirteenth century when a series of earthquakes shook the valley in which it is located, opening cracks in the ground. After its creation, it reportedly erupted every three hours with thunderous jets of water and steam shooting 200 to 260 feet (60 to 80 meters) above the ground.

The geyser continued to erupt on a regular basis until the beginning of the nineteenth century. From then on, it erupted at progressively longer intervals until 1916, when it stopped completely. It came to life briefly in 1935, but since then has not erupted on its own accord.

Geologists believe that part of the reason Geysir has stopped erupting is due to the accumulation of rocks and other matter thrown into its vent by tourists over the centuries. These objects most likely damaged the geyser's plumbing system. Despite the inactivity of the Great Geysir, the surrounding area remains quite active. Many smaller hot springs surround the geyser, and nearby is another geyser, named Stokkur. It erupts roughly every 10 minutes, shooting a column of water 65 to 100 feet (20 to 30 meters) above its vent.

Hot Springs National Park, Arkansas

Covering more than 5,550 acres (2,220 hectares) of land in Arkansas, the Hot Springs National Park contains 47 natural hot springs. To protect and preserve these springs, the U.S. Congress designated the area a reservation in 1832, and then made it a national park in 1921.

OPPOSITE Considered the most famous geyser in the world, Old Faithful, in Yellowstone National Park, Wyoming, shoots water and steam up to 184 feet about every 90 minutes. **PHOTOGRAPH REPRODUCED BY PERMISSION OF THE CORBIS CORPORATION.**

Unlike the water in many other hot springs, the water in the springs of Hot Springs National Park is not heated by underground magma. There is no evidence that volcanic activity has occurred in this area. Instead, the rainwater that feeds the springs has traveled downward to depths between 2,000 and 8,000 feet (610 and 2,438 meters). Here, as groundwater, it is heated by the naturally hot rocks. The heated water then rises quickly—the journey upward takes about one year—through cracks and faults to emerge as hot springs. The total amount of water that comes out of the springs averages about 850,000 gallons (3,217,250 liters) a day.

At the surface, the average temperature of the water in the hot springs is 147°F (64°C). What is noteworthy about the water is that it is sterile: no bacteria are found in it.

Old Faithful, Yellowstone National Park, Wyoming

Although not the biggest or the most regular, Old Faithful in the Upper Geyser Basin in Yellowstone National Park is considered by many to be the world's most famous geyser. It was named in 1870 by members of the Washburn Expedition, the first official expedition to Yellowstone (the park became the world's first national park in 1872). They were awed by the geyser's size and the frequency of its eruptions.

Its eruptions, which last from 1.5 to 5 minutes, spray water and steam from 90 to 184 feet (27 to 56 meters) above the ground. The intervals between eruptions range from 35 to 120 minutes, depending on the length of the eruption. The shorter the eruption, the shorter the interval until the next eruption. At one point, the average interval was every 76 minutes, but earthquakes in the area in the winter in the late twentieth century changed that. At present, the geyser erupts on average every 90 minutes or so, spouting from 3,700 to 8,400 gallons (14,005 to 31,794 liters) of water that has a temperature underground of 204°F (96°C).

Old Faithful is a cone geyser. By measuring the geyserite deposited around the vent of the geyser, scientists estimate that Old Faithful is approximately 300 years old. Before that, the geyser existed as a regular hot spring for several hundred years.

For More Information

Books

Brimner, Larry Dane. *Geysers*. New York: Children's Press, 2000.

Bryan, T. Scott. *The Geysers of Yellowstone*. Third ed. Boulder, CO: University Press of Colorado, 1995.

Downs, Sandra. *Earth's Fiery Fury*. Brookfield, CT: Twenty-First Century Books, 2000.

Gallant, Roy A. *Geysers: When Earth Roars.* New York: Scholastic Library Publishing, 1997.

Web Sites

"Geothermal Energy and Hydrothermal Activity: Fumaroles, Hot Springs, Geysers." *U.S. Geological Survey.* http://vulcan.wr.usgs.gov/Glossary/ThermalActivity/description_thermal_activity.html (accessed on September 1, 2003).

The Geyser Observation and Study Association. http://www.geyserstudy.org/ (accessed on September 1, 2003).

"Geysers, Fumaroles, and Hot Springs." *U.S. Geological Survey.* http://pubs.usgs.gov/gip/volc/geysers.html (accessed on September 1, 2003).

"Infrared Yellowstone Gallery." *Infrared Processing and Analysis Center, California Institute of Technology.* http://coolcosmos.ipac.caltech.edu/image_galleries/ir_yellowstone/ (accessed on September 1, 2003).

"World Geyser Fields." *Department of Geography and Geology, Western Kentucky University.* http://www.uweb.ucsb.edu/~glennon/geysers/ (accessed on September 1, 2003).

WyoJones' Geyser Site. http://www.wyojones.com/jonesy/geysers.htm (accessed on September 1, 2003).

Glacial landforms and features

During the last Ice Age, which ended approximately 10,000 years ago, 32 percent of Earth's land area was covered with glaciers. At present, glaciers cover roughly 10 percent of the land area. A vast majority of that glacial ice overlies much of the continent of Antarctica. Most of the rest covers a great portion of Greenland; a small percentage is found in places such as Alaska, the Canadian Arctic, Patagonia, New Zealand, the Himalayan Mountains, and the Alps.

Glaciers are not landforms. The action of glaciers, however, creates landforms. It is a process known as glaciation. Glacial ice is an active agent of erosion, which is the gradual wearing away of Earth surfaces through the action of wind and water. Glaciers move, and as they do, they scour the landscape, "carving" out landforms. They also deposit rocky material they have picked up, creating even more features. The work of present-day glaciers, however, is slow and confined to certain areas of the planet. Less obvious but far more reaching has been the work of Ice Age glaciers. Many of the distinctive features of the northern landscapes of North America and Europe were formed by glaciers that once covered almost one-third of the planet's land surface.

The shape of the land

A glacier is a large body of ice that formed on land from the compaction and recrystallization of snow, survives year to year, and shows some sign of movement downhill due to gravity. Two types of glaciers exist: relatively small glaciers that form in high elevations near the tops of mountains are called alpine or mountain glaciers; glaciers that form over large areas of continents close to the poles (the North and South Poles; the extreme northernmost and southernmost points on the globe) are called continental glaciers or ice sheets. Two continental glaciers are found on Earth: one covers 85 percent of Greenland in the Northern

Words to Know

Ablation zone: The area of a glacier where mass is lost through melting or evaporation at a greater rate than snow and ice accumulate.

Accumulation zone: The area of a glacier where mass is increased through snowfall at a greater rate than snow and ice is lost through ablation.

Alpine glacier: A relatively small glacier that forms in high elevations near the tops of mountains.

Arête: A sharp-edged ridge of rock formed between adjacent cirque glaciers.

Basal sliding: The sliding of a glacier over the ground on a layer of water.

Cirque: A bowl-shaped depression carved out of a mountain by an alpine glacier.

Continental glacier: A glacier that forms over large areas of continents close to the poles.

Crevasse: A deep, nearly vertical crack that develops in the upper portion of glacier ice.

Erosion: The gradual wearing away of Earth surfaces through the action of wind and water.

Erratic: A large boulder that a glacier deposits on a surface made of different rock.

Esker: A long, snakelike ridge of sediment deposited by a stream that ran under or within a glacier.

Firn: The granular ice formed by the recrystallization of snow; also known as névé.

Fjord: A deep glacial trough submerged with seawater.

Glacial drift: A general term for all material transported and deposited directly by or from glacial ice.

Glacial polish: The smooth and shiny surfaces that are produced on rocks underneath a glacier by material carried in the base of that glacier.

Glacial surge: The rapid forward movement of a glacier.

Glacial trough: A U-shaped valley carved out of a V-shaped stream valley by the movement of a valley glacier.

Glaciation: The transformation of the landscape through the action of glaciers.

Glacier: A large body of ice that formed on land by the compaction and recrystallization of snow, survives year to year, and shows some sign of movement downhill due to gravity.

Ground moraine: A continuous layer of till deposited beneath a steadily retreating glacier.

Hemisphere and the other covers more than 95 percent of Antarctica in the Southern Hemisphere.

Both types of glaciers create landforms through erosion. These erosional features may be as large as the Great Lakes of North America or as small as scratches left in pebbles. As a glacier moves, it scours away material underneath it, plucking up rocks, some of which may be house-sized boulders. This material then becomes embedded in the ice at the base of a glacier. As the glacier continues to move, the embedded material abrades or scrapes the rock underneath. The slow scraping and grinding produces a fine-grained material known as rock flour. It also produces long parallel scratches and grooves known as striations in the underlying rocks. Because they are aligned parallel

Hanging valley: A shallow glacial trough that leads into the side of a larger, main glacial trough.

Horn: A high mountain peak that forms when the walls of three or more glacial cirques intersect.

Internal flow: The movement of ice inside a glacier through the deformation and realignment of ice crystals; also known as creep.

Kame: A steep-sided, conical mound or hill formed of glacial drift that is created when sediment is washed into a depression on the top surface of a glacier and then deposited on the ground below when the glacier melts away.

Kettle: A shallow, bowl-shaped depression formed when a large block of glacial ice breaks away from the main glacier and is buried beneath glacial till, then melts. If the depression fills with water, it is known as a kettle lake.

Lateral moraine: A moraine deposited along the side of a valley glacier.

Medial moraine: A moraine formed when two adjacent glaciers flow into each other and their lateral moraines are caught in the middle of the joined glacier.

Meltwater: The water from melted snow or ice.

Moraine: A general term for a ridge or mound of till deposited by a glacier.

Piedmont glacier: A valley glacier that flows out of a mountainous area onto a gentle slope or plain and spreads out over the surrounding terrain.

Rock flour: Fine-grained rock material produced when a glacier abrades or scrapes rock beneath it.

Snow line: The elevation above which snow can form and remain all year.

Striations: The long, parallel scratches and grooves produced in rocks underneath a glacier as it moves over them.

Tarn: A small lake that fills the central depression in a cirque.

Terminal moraine: A moraine found near the terminus of a glacier; also known as an end moraine.

Terminus: The leading edge of a glacier; also known as the glacier snout.

Till: A random mixture of finely crushed rock, sand, pebbles, and boulders deposited by a glacier.

Valley glacier: An alpine glacier flowing downward through a preexisting stream valley.

to the direction of ice flow, glacial striations help geologists determine the flow path of former glaciers. Another small-scale erosional feature is glacial polish. This is a smooth and shiny surface produced on rocks underneath a glacier when material encased in the ice abrades the rocks like fine sandpaper.

Moving ice sculpts a variety of landforms out of the landscape. Larger-scale erosional features include bowl-shaped, steep-walled depressions carved out of the side of mountains. These depressions are called cirques (pronounced SIRKS), and the relatively small alpine glaciers that fill them are called cirque glaciers. If the glacier melts and a small lake fills the central depression in a cirque, that lake is known as a tarn. Two or more glacial cirques may form on a mountainside, eroding away the rock between them to create a steep-sided, sharp-edged ridge known as an arête (pronounced ah-RHET). When the walls of three or more glacial cirques meet, they may form a high mountain peak known as a horn.

When a cirque glacier expands outward and flows downward through a stream valley that already exists, it becomes a valley glacier. Through erosion, valley glaciers turn V-shaped stream valleys into U-shaped glacial troughs. Smaller valley glaciers, known as tributary glaciers, may form alongside a main valley glacier and eventually flow into it. The shallower glacial troughs created by these glaciers are known as hanging valleys. A valley glacier that flows out of a mountainous area onto a gentle slope or plain and spreads out over the surrounding terrain is a piedmont glacier. A valley glacier may flow all the way to a coastline, carving out a narrow glacial trough. If the glacier melts and the valley fills with seawater, it is known as a fjord (pronounced fee-ORD). Although prominent along the west coast of Norway, fjords are also found along the coasts of Alaska, British Columbia, Chile, Greenland, New Zealand, and Scotland.

Glaciers leave their mark on the landscape not only through erosion, but also through deposition. Deposition involves carrying loose materials from one area and leaving, or depositing, these materials in another area. Depositional features are created by the release of rocky material from a glacier. They vary widely in scale and form. All sediment (rock debris ranging from clay to boulders) deposited as a result of glacial erosion is called glacial drift. Like a stream, a glacier picks up and carries sediment particles of various sizes. Unlike a stream, a glacier can carry part of that sediment load on its bottom, its sides, or its top (sediment on top has fallen onto the glacier from the valley walls). Another difference between the two is that when a stream deposits its load of sediment, it does so in order of size and weight: large, heavy particles are deposited first, followed by particles that are increasingly smaller and lighter. When a glacier deposits sediment, there is no such order. The particles are unsorted, with large and small particles mixed together. This random mixture of finely crushed rock, sand, pebbles, and boulders deposited by a glacier is referred to as till.

Since a glacier can carry rocks for great distances before depositing them, those rocks generally differ from the surrounding native rocks in that area. In fact, because they are derived from a very large area eroded by a glacier, glacial deposits contain the widest variety of rock types. A glacially deposited large boulder that differs in composition from the rocks around it is called an erratic.

A deposit of till that forms a ridge or mound is called a moraine (meh-RAIN). Moraines deposited along the sides of alpine glaciers are called lateral moraines. When two valley glaciers converge to create a single larger glacier, their opposing lateral moraines merge to form a ridge that

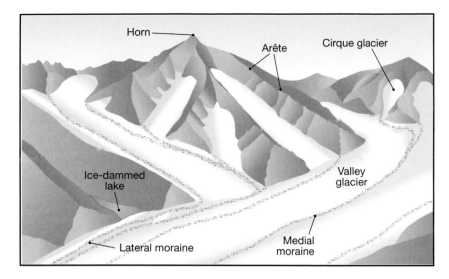

Major features of glaciation, or the action of glaciers on a landscape.

In image: Horn, Arête, Cirque glacier, Ice-dammed lake, Valley glacier, Lateral moraine, Medial moraine

runs down the middle of the new glacier. This is a medial moraine. A moraine deposited at the leading edge of a glacier, marking its farthest advance, is a terminal or end moraine. Finally, a continuous layer of till deposited beneath a steadily retreating glacier is a ground moraine.

Another common glacial landform is the drumlin. This tear-drop-shaped hill forms underneath a glacier. The tail of the drumlin points in the direction of the ice movement. Geologists are unsure exactly how drumlins form, whether a glacier scrapes up material beneath it or deposits material it already carries or a combination of both. Drumlins may be quite large, measuring up to 200 feet (60 meters) in height and 0.6 mile (1 kilometer) in length.

As a glacier melts, it produces meltwater that flows on top, within, and underneath the glacier through channels. This meltwater moves large quantities of sediment from the glacier. At the leading edge of the glacier, also known as the terminus or glacier snout, the meltwater emerges in large streams that carry it away from the glacier. The sediment in the meltwater is then deposited, forming a broad, sweeping plain called an outwash plain. Since the sediment was carried in water, it is deposited in a sorted manner, with the largest particles first and the smallest particles last. If a glacier melts and retreats, curving, snakelike ridges of sediment may mark the former locations of streams that existed under the glacier. These long, twisting ridges are called eskers.

Two other features that result from the melting of glaciers are kames and kettles. As a glacier begins to melt, a depression may form on its top surface, filling with water and sediment. When the glacier finally melts away, the sediment is set down on the surface of the ground, forming a

Loess

Loess (pronounced LUSS; a German word meaning "loose") is a deposit of fine, yellowish-gray, silty sediment. Composed of mineral particles finer than sand but coarser than dust or clay, loess forms fertile topsoils. Areas with large loess deposits are found in the central and northwestern United States, in central and eastern Europe, and in eastern China.

The majority of loess was formed by the action of glaciers and wind (some loess comes from the transport of sediment from desert areas). After the last ice age, meltwater streams from the retreating continental glaciers transported vast amounts of rock flour and other fine sediment away from the glaciers. Strong winds blowing off the glaciers (because glacial ice cools the air and cold air moves to lower elevations at the front of the glacier) picked up the fine sediment and carried it far beyond the outwash plains before it was deposited.

Since loess is transported in the air, it is very well sorted, and is mostly silt combined with a small amount of clay. Loess is generally deposited as a blanket over everything, both hills and valleys. It is often removed by wind and water to fill up basins and depressions.

steep-sided, conical mound or hill known as a kame. A kettle forms when a large chunk of ice separates from the main glacier. Buried by glacial till, the ice then melts, leaving a depression in the landscape. This eventually becomes filled with water, forming a kettle lake.

Forces and changes: Construction and destruction

Glaciers are moving ice. They can range in size from small patches to ice sheets covering millions of square miles. The world's largest alpine glacier is the Siachen Glacier in the Karakoram Mountains of Pakistan. Measuring 47 miles (75 kilometers) in length, it contains more than 13.6 cubic miles (56.7 cubic kilometers) of ice. The Antarctic ice sheet is the largest single mass of ice on Earth. It covers an area of almost 5.4 million square miles (14 million square kilometers) and contains over 7 million cubic miles (29 million cubic kilometers) of ice.

Glacial formation

A glacier does not start out as a glacier. All that ice began to form when snow—delicate, feathery crystals of ice—fell in areas above the snow line, the elevation above which snow can form and remain all year. It takes snow on top of snow on top of more snow to create a glacier; it also takes a long time. On average, 10 feet (3 meters) of snow will turn into 1 foot (0.3 meter) of ice. In polar regions, where annual snowfall is

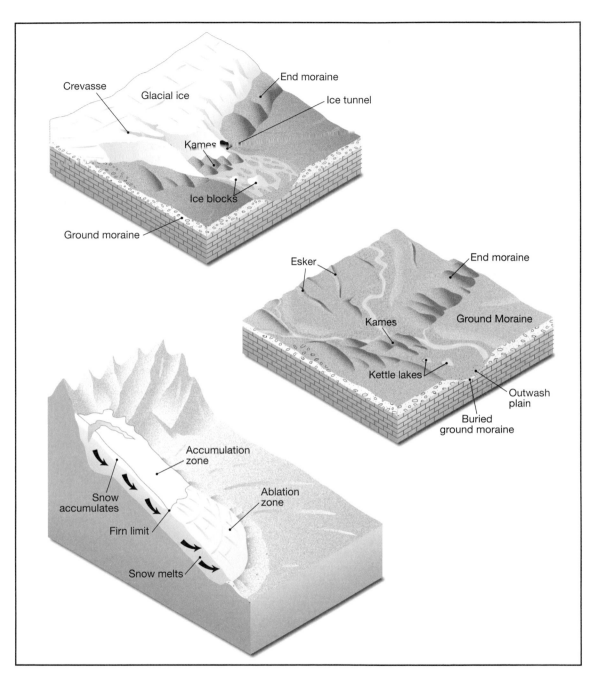

Glacial effects and features.

generally very low because the air is too cold to hold much moisture, it may take snow about 1,000 years to turn into ice.

In time, if snow does not melt but is buried beneath additional layers of snow, it will begin to compress. This forces the snow crystals to recrystallize, forming grains similar in size and shape to cane sugar. As new snow piles on top and the snow below becomes further compressed, the grains grow larger and the air spaces between them become smaller. Over a short period of time, perhaps the span of two winters, the compressed snow turns into a granular material known as firn or névé (pronounced nay-VAY). The density (amount of mass in a given volume) of regular snow is about 10 percent that of water. The density of firn is about 50 percent that of water. Once the thickness of the overlying snow exceeds about 165 feet (50 meters), the firn turns into a solid mass of glacial ice.

Additions to a glacier's mass are called accumulation; losses through melting, erosion, or evaporation are called ablation (pronounced ah-BLAY-shun). A glacier may be divided into two distinct zones. Where snow and ice accumulate faster than they melt away or evaporate is the accumulation zone; where melting and evaporation occur faster than accumulation is the ablation zone. The upper part of a glacier is its accumulation zone, while the lower part is its ablation zone. The boundary between the two zones is called the firn limit.

Over a period of years, depending on the amount of snowfall and seasonal temperatures, a glacier may gain more mass than it loses. If this occurs, the terminus of the glacier will likely advance. If the opposite happens, with the glacier losing more mass than it gains, its terminus will likely retreat. Thus, depending on the balance between accumulation and ablation, a glacier may grow or shrink.

Ice flow

A glacier always moves in the same direction whether it is advancing or retreating. It moves to lower elevations under the force of gravity by two different processes: internal flow and basal sliding. The glacial ice beneath the firn in a glacier is so dense and under such pressure that it begins to behave like thick tar or what geologists term "plastic." The individual ice crystals in this area respond to pressure and the force of gravity by deforming yet again. They are forced into the same orientation or direction, all realigning parallel to the direction of flow. Like cards in a deck of playing cards, they then slide over and past one another. Glacial movement through internal flow, also known as creep, is very slow: on average, it measures only an inch or two (a few centimeters) a day. In a valley glacier, ice in the upper central part moves faster than ice at the sides, where it is in contact with the valley walls.

Confined by high pressures, ice deep in a glacier does not crack during internal flow. However, near the surface of the glacier where there is less pressure, the ice is brittle. When the lower portion of a glacier moves by internal flow, especially over abrupt changes in slope, large cracks may

Ice Ages

Ice ages were periods in Earth's history when vast glaciers covered large portions of the planet's surface. Earth's average annual temperature varies constantly from year to year, from decade to decade, and from century to century. During some periods, that average annual temperature has dropped low enough to allow fields of ice to grow and cover large areas of Earth. Annual variations of only a few degrees can result in the formation of extensive continental glaciers.

Over the last 2.5 million years, about twenty-four ice ages have occurred. This means that Earth's average annual temperature shifted upwards and downwards about two dozen times during that period. In each case, an episode of significant cooling was followed by an episode of significant warming, called an interglacial period, after which cooling took place once more. At present, Earth is in an interglacial period.

The exact causes for ice ages have not been proven. Scientists believe that ice ages are the result of a complicated interaction between such things as variations in the Sun's energy output, the varying distance of Earth from the Sun, variations in the tilt of Earth's axis, the changing position and height of the continents, changing oceanic circulation, and changes in the composition of the atmosphere.

develop in the upper 150 feet (45 meters) or so of ice. These deep, nearly vertical cracks are called crevasses (pronounced kri-VASS-ez).

Glaciers in polar regions are frozen to the ground and move only through internal flow. Glaciers elsewhere are normally warm enough at their bases to have a layer of water form between their ice and the ground. The water reduces friction by lubricating the ground and allowing the glacier to slide on its bed in what is called basal sliding. This second type of glacial movement occurs because high pressure reduces the temperature at which ice will melt. Ice underneath a 7,220-foot (2,200-meter) glacier will melt at roughly 29°F (–1.6°C), rather than at 32°F (0°C). The thicker the glacier, the greater the pressure at its base, and the lower the temperature at which its ice will melt.

Other factors may also contribute to basal sliding. Because ice acts like a blanket, a glacier traps heat that escapes from the surface of Earth. Although not much, this heat may be enough to raise the temperature of ice at the base of a glacier to a little above the pressure-melting point. Meltwater from the top or inside a glacier may also make its way down through cracks and channels to the glacier's base, contributing to the layer of water formed there. Glacial movement due to basal sliding may be ten times faster than that due to internal flow. Because of this, basal sliding plays an

The Literary Landscape

"These islands of ice and black basalt, now and then tinged russet or blue by oozings of iron or copper, rise over 600 meters. Their hearts are locked under deep glaciers, a crystal desert forever frozen in terms of our short life spans, but transient in their own time scale. Sometimes one sees only the cloud-marbled glacial fields, high in the sun above hidden mountain slopes and sea fog, Elysian plains that seem as insubstantial as vapor. The interiors of the glaciers, glimpsed through crevasses, are neon blue. Sliding imperceptibly on their bellies, the glaciers carve their own valleys through the rock, and when they pass over rough terrain they have the appearance of frozen rapids, which is in fact what they are, cascading at a rate of a centimeter a day."

—**David C. Campbell,** *The Crystal Desert: Summers in Antarctica,* **1992.**

important role in how much a glacier erodes a landscape and creates landforms.

On rare occasions, an alpine glacier may unexpectedly surge downslope, moving at a rate of 165 to 330 feet (50 to 100 meters) per day. This results in a jumbled mass of ice along the terminus of the glacier and many crevasses along its top. Although geologists do not completely understand the reasons for glacial surging, they believe it may be caused by a buildup of meltwater at the base of a glacier that reduces the normal friction and allows unusually fast basal sliding. The fastest-recorded glacial surge was that of the Kutiah Glacier in northern Pakistan. Over a three-month period in 1953, the glacier slid more than 7.5 miles (12 kilometers), averaging about 367 feet (112 meters) per day.

Through the combination of internal flow and basal sliding, glaciers move over a landscape, scraping and plucking the rock surfaces over which they move. They transport unsorted sediment both internally and on their surfaces. During warmer periods, a glacier may lose part of its mass, its ice turning to meltwater, which carries sediment away from the terminus of the glacier. Even as a glacier's terminus retreats, the flow of ice in the glacier continues to move downward under the influence of gravity.

Scientific measurements at the beginning of the twenty-first century showed that most glaciers worldwide were retreating. Glaciers in the Himalayan Mountains were wasting away the quickest. Scientists who conducted the research found a connection between increasing temperatures around the world and the glacial retreat. It is known that over the last 100 years, global sea levels have risen 4 to 10 inches (10 to 25 centimeters). Scientists estimate that the melting of glaciers has contributed 1 to 2 inches (2.5 to 5 centimeters) to that rise.

Spotlight on famous forms

Glacier National Park, Montana

Located in northwestern Montana on the border between the United States and Canada are 1,013,572 acres (410,497 hectares) of pristine

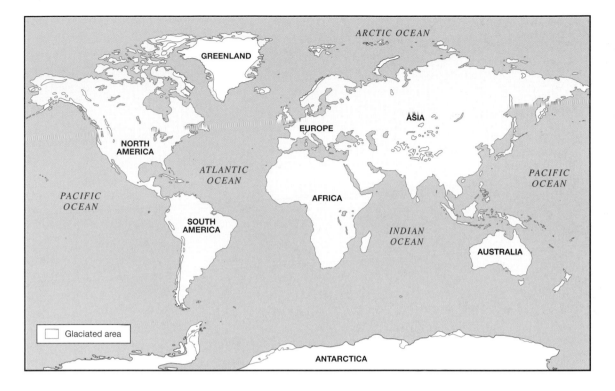

wilderness. Glacier National Park, established in 1910 as the country's tenth national park, contains some fifty glaciers and more than two hundred glacier-fed lakes. The valleys and other geologic features of the park were all eroded and carved by the action of glaciers over the last two billion years. Several times over the past two million years, huge glaciers carved the mountains and valleys and then retreated, leaving a newly sculpted landscape. The most recent continental glacier that covered the upper section of North America retreated over ten thousand years ago. The fifty alpine glaciers in the park formed during the last few thousand years.

The park is filled with many glacial features: arêtes, cirques, hanging valleys, horns, and moraines. Among the more famous ones are Mount Reynolds, a glacial horn; Garden Wall, a towering arête that extends for miles; and the U-shaped St. Mary Valley.

Matterhorn, Switzerland

One of the most recognizable mountains in the world, the Matterhorn in the Pennine Alps on the border between Switzerland and Italy rises some 14,700 feet (4,480 meters). First successfully climbed in 1865, it is celebrated for its distinctive shape. The mountain is a classic example of

Map of glaciers around the world. Glaciers cover roughly 10 percent of Earth's land area. A vast majority of that, 90 percent, overlies the continent of Antarctica.

a horn. Eroded by cirques, its steep sides meet in arêtes that lead to the hornlike, pointed peak.

The Alps mountain system in southern-central Europe curves in a great arc for approximately 500 miles (800 kilometers). It runs from the Mediterranean Sea up along the borders and adjacent regions of France, Italy, Switzerland, Germany, and Austria, before ending in Slovenia. The Alps was the first mountain system to be studied extensively by geologists. Many of the geologic terms associated with mountains and glaciers originated in those studies.

Walden Pond, Massachusetts

Walden Pond, the deepest lake in Massachusetts, lies in the northeast part of the state near the city of Concord. It is a kettle lake, created about ten thousand years ago when continental ice from the last ice age began to retreat. A huge block of that glacial ice broke off and remained behind, surrounded at it base by sand and gravel deposited by meltwater streams. The block melted over a period of about two hundred years, forming a steep-sided basin that filled with water. The current shape of the pond, with its steep sides, coves along its margins, and two deep areas, reflects the shape of the original block of ice. The current maximum depth of the pond is 103 feet (31 meters). The clear water that fills the lake comes from precipitation and groundwater (freshwater lying within the uppermost parts of Earth's crust, filling the pore spaces in soil and fractured rock).

The lake is famous because American writer Henry David Thoreau (1817–1862) lived along its shores between 1845 and 1847. While there, he wrote *Walden, or Life in the Woods* (published in 1854). In this work, a series of essays, Thoreau combined writing on transcendental philosophy with observations of aquatic ecology and aspects of limnology, the study of lakes. He also championed the value of living close to nature. Because of this highly influential work, many people consider Walden Pond and the area around it to be the birthplace of the American conservation movement.

In 1965, the U.S. National Park Service designated Walden Pond as a National Historic Landmark.

For More Information

Books

Benn, Douglas I., and David J. A. Evans. *Glaciers and Glaciation.* London, England: Edward Arnold, 1998.

Bennett, Matthew R., and Neil F. Glasser. *Glacial Geology: Ice Sheets and Landforms.* New York: John Wiley and Sons, 1996.

Erickson, Jon. *Glacial Geology: How Ice Shapes the Land.* New York: Facts on File, 1996.

Llewellyn, Claire. *Glaciers*. Barrington, IL: Heinemann Library, 2000.

Post, Austin, and Edward R. Lachapelle. *Glacier Ice*. Revised ed. Seattle: University of Washington Press, 2000.

Web Sites

"All About Glaciers." *National Snow and Ice Data Center.* http://nsidc.org/glaciers/ (accessed on September 1, 2003).

"Glacial Landforms." *South Central Service Cooperative.* http://www.scsc.k12.ar.us/2001Outwest/PacificEcology/Projects/HendricksR/default.htm (accessed on September 1, 2003).

"Glaciers and Glacial Geology." *Montana State University-Bozeman.* http://gemini.oscs.montana.edu/~geol445/hyperglac/index.htm (accessed on September 1, 2003).

Glaciers, Rivers of Ice. http://members.aol.com/scipioiv/glmain.html (accessed on September 1, 2003).

"Illustrated Glossary of Alpine Glacial Landforms." *Department of Geography and Geology, University of Wisconsin-Stevens Point.* http://www.uwsp.edu/geo/faculty/lemke/alpine_glacial_glossary/glossary.html (accessed on September 1, 2003).

Landslide and other gravity movements

1
2
3
4
5
6
7
8
9
10
11
12
13
14
15
16
17
18
19
20
21
22

Gravity is the physical force of attraction between any two objects in the universe. One of the four fundamental forces (the others are electromagnetism and the strong and weak forces), gravity affects all objects on Earth. From the largest mountains to the smallest grains of sand, gravity pulls everything in a direction toward the center of the planet. As long as material remains on a flat surface, one that is parallel to Earth's surface, gravity will not cause it to move. When material is on a slope and conditions are right, however, gravity will cause it to fall, slide, flow, slump, or creep downward.

That downhill movement of soil, rocks, mud, and other debris can be either slow or fast. Large amounts that move quickly are perhaps the most widespread geologic hazard. Each year in the United States, ground failures of various sorts cause between twenty-five and fifty deaths and roughly $1.5 billion in economic loss. In less-developed nations, where poorly constructed buildings house many people in areas prone to ground failures, the death tolls and amount of property damage are much higher.

The shape of the land

Geologists use the term mass wasting to describe the spontaneous movement of Earth material down a slope in response to gravity. This does not include material transported downward by streams, winds, or glaciers. Mass wasting plays an important role in the overall process of erosion, which is the gradual wearing away of Earth surfaces through the action of wind and water. Through mass wasting, material from higher elevations is moved to lower elevations where streams, glaciers, and wind pick it up and move it to even lower elevations. Mass wasting occurs continuously on all slopes. While some mass-wasting processes act very slowly, others occur very suddenly. The general term landslide is used to describe all relatively rapid forms of mass wasting.

Landslide in San Salvador, El Salvador, resulting from a powerful earthquake. **PHOTOGRAPH REPRODUCED BY PERMISSION OF THE CORBIS CORPORATION.**

Mass wasting may be divided into two broad categories: slope failures and flows. Slope failures occur when debris moves downslope as the result of a sudden failure on a steep slope or cliff. Flows occur when a loose mixture of debris, water, and air move downslope in a fluidlike manner. Each of these categories may be further divided into various types: Slope failures include falls, slides, and slumps; flows include mudflows, debris flows, solifluction (pronounced so-lih-FLUK-shun), debris avalanches, earthflows, and creep. Flows may be grouped according to the amount of water present in the particular flow. Mudflows, debris flows, and solifluction are labeled slurry flows. These contain between 20 and 40 percent water. Debris avalanches, earthflows, and creep are granular or dry flows, which contain up to 20 percent water.

A fall is a sudden, steep drop of rock fragments or debris. A rockfall commonly occurs on a steep cliff and may involve a single rock or a mass of rocks. As a rock falls down, it may plummet freely through the air or may strike and loosen other rocks in the cliff face. At the base of the cliff, the rock fragments accumulate in a sloping pile known as a talus (pronounced TAY-less). The largest rocks in the pile tend to be located the farthest from the cliff face because of their greater size and momentum. Debris falls differ from rockfalls only in that they involve a mixture of soil, rocks, and vegetation.

In contrast to a fall, material in a slide maintains contact with the slope down which it moves. That material could be a mass of rocks or debris. Piles of talus are common where rock or debris slides end. A rock slide involving tons of material may reach a speed exceeding 100 miles (161 kilometers) per hour.

A slump is the downward movement of a block of material on a curved surface, one shaped like a spoon. Instead of sliding downward parallel to the surface of the slope, a slump block rotates backward toward the slope in a series of curving downward and outward movements, creating a series of steplike depressions. A bulge of material, known as a toe, develops at the base of the slope. At the head of the slump, a scalloped hollow is left in the slope. A slump generally does not travel far, unlike a fall or a slide, normally moving at a pace of 7 feet (2.1 meters) per day or slower.

The most common, the most liquid, and the fastest type of flow is a mudflow. A mixture primarily of the smallest silt and clay particles and water, a mudflow has the consistency of newly mixed concrete. It can travel down a slope as fast as 55 miles (88 kilometers) per hour and have enough force to pick up and carry along debris the size of boulders, cars, trees, and houses. Mudflows can travel for great distances over gently sloping terrain. When they reach valley floors, mudflows spread out, depositing a thin layer of mud mixed with boulders. A type of mudflow produced by a volcanic eruption is called a lahar (pronounced LAH-hahr). A mixture of volcanic ash, rocks,

Words to Know

Angle of repose: The steepest angle at which loose material on a slope remains motionless.

Bedrock: The general term for the solid rock that underlies the soil.

Chemical weathering: The process by which chemical reactions alter the chemical makeup of rocks and minerals.

Creep: The extremely slow, almost continuous movement of soil and other material downslope.

Debris avalanche: The extremely rapid downward movement of rocks, soil, mud, and other debris mixed with air and water.

Debris flow: A mixture of water and clay, silt, sand, and rock fragments that flows rapidly down steep slopes.

Earthflow: The downward movement of water-saturated, clay-rich soil on a moderate slope.

Erosion: The gradual wearing away of Earth surfaces through the action of wind and water.

Fall: A sudden, steep drop of rock fragments or debris.

Flow: The downward movement of a loose mixture of debris, water, and air that moves in a fluidlike manner.

Granular flow: A flow that contains up to 20 percent water.

Gravity: The physical force of attraction between any two objects in the universe.

Lahar: A mudflow composed of volcanic ash, rocks, and water produced by a volcanic eruption.

Landslide: A general term used to describe all relatively rapid forms of mass wasting.

Mass wasting: The spontaneous movement of material down a slope in response to gravity.

Mechanical weathering: The process by which a rock or mineral is broken down into smaller fragments without altering its chemical makeup.

Mudflow: A mixture primarily made of the smallest silt and clay particles and water that has the consistency of newly mixed concrete and that flows quickly down slopes.

Regolith: The layer of loose, uncemented rocks and rock fragments of various size that lies beneath the soil and above the bedrock.

Shear stress: The force of gravity acting on an object on a slope, pulling it downward in a direction parallel to the slope.

Slide: The movement of a mass of rocks or debris down a slope.

Slope failure: A type of mass wasting that occurs when debris moves downward as the result of a sudden failure on a steep slope or cliff.

Slump: The downward movement of blocks of material on a curved surface.

Slurry flow: A flow that contains between 20 and 40 percent water.

Solifluction: A form of mass wasting that occurs in relatively cold regions in which waterlogged soil flows very slowly down a slope.

Talus: A sloping pile of rock fragments lying at the base of the cliff or steep slope from which they have broken off; also known as scree.

Weathering: The process by which rocks and minerals are broken down at or near Earth's surface.

and water from melted snow and glaciers around the volcanic crater, a lahar may be very hot. Traveling down the steep side of a volcano at speeds approaching 200 miles (322 kilometers) per hour, a lahar can flow for great distances, burying everything it encounters.

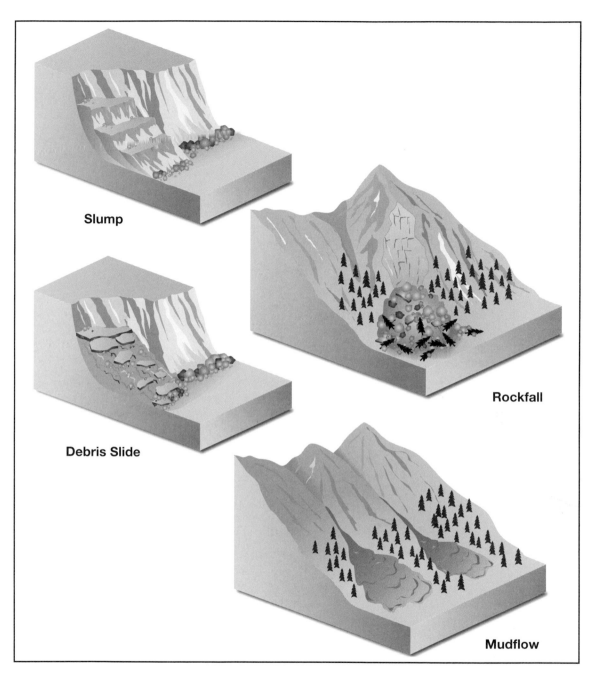

Slump

Rockfall

Debris Slide

Mudflow

A mixture of water and clay, silt, sand, and rock fragments (more than half of the particles are larger than sand), a debris flow travels at a slower speed than a mudflow, usually up to about 25 miles (40 kilometers) per hour. At this velocity, a debris flow still has enough energy to

Some of the major forms of mass wasting, or the spontaneous movement of material down a slope in response to gravity.

pick up and transport large rocks, boulders, trees, and other material in its path. This type of flow generally occurs on steep slopes that have little or no vegetation. Traveling downward, the material in a debris flow tends to mix with more water and even air. Studies have shown that debris flows gain speed because they actually ride on a cushion of air as they flow downslope.

The slowest type of slurry flow is called solifluction. This form of mass wasting occurs in relatively cold regions where short summers thaw the uppermost layers of soil, generally the top 3 feet (1 meter). Below this remains a layer of permanently frozen soil called permafrost through which the water does not drain. Water-saturated and weak, the upper layers flow very slowly downslope at a rate of 0.2 to 5.9 inches (0.5 to 15 centimeters) per year, forming distinct lobes (rounded segments).

The fastest type of granular flow is the debris avalanche. The term avalanche is generally applied to any fast-moving downward flow of any type of material. Similar to an avalanche of snow, a debris avalanche is an extremely rapid downward movement of rocks, soil, mud, and other debris mixed with air and water. Common in areas with steep slopes, debris avalanches usually result from the complete collapse of a mountainous slope, often triggered by earthquakes and volcanic eruptions. They move downward through avalanche chutes (channel-like depressions along which an avalanche has moved), reaching speeds over 300 miles (480 kilometers) per hour. Debris avalanches can travel for considerable distances along relatively gentle slopes.

Another type of granular flow is an earthflow, which usually occurs when clay-rich soil has become saturated by heavy rains. The material in an earthflow is coarser and less fluid than that in a mudflow and finer and more fluid than that in a debris flow. Although it may move at a variety of speeds and over varying distances, an earthflow generally moves slower and travels a shorter distance than a mudflow. Slow earthflows move in starts and stops, covering only several feet per year. This type of flow normally has an hourglass shape. A bowl or depression forms at the head where the unstable material collects and flows downward. It narrows in its central area before widening once again at the base of the slope.

Creep is the extremely slow, almost continuous movement of soil and other material downslope. Most creep movement is less than 0.4 inch (1 centimeter) per year. Occurring on almost all slopes, it is the most widespread and costliest type of mass wasting in terms of total material moved and monetary damage caused. Although creep cannot be witnessed, evidence of the movement can be seen on hillslopes in curved tree trucks and leaning fence posts, telephone poles, and gravestones.

Submarine Flows

Storms or earthquakes may trigger flows of water and sediment down a continental slope, the steeply sloping region of the continental margin (the submerged outer edge of a continent) that extends downward to the ocean basin. As the material begins to move down the slope, it gathers speed and mixes with water to form turbidity currents. Because they are heavier than the surrounding water, the currents are pulled downward by gravity. Flowing at speeds of up to 50 miles (80 kilometers) per hour, the currents gather more sediment by scouring the slope as they travel downward. When they come to the base of the slope, the currents slow and the sediments settle on ocean basin, forming a fanlike deposit. (For more information on turbidity currents, see the **Continental margin** entry.)

Forces and changes: Construction and destruction

Mass wasting occurs throughout the world, continually sculpting the landscape. The areas at greatest risk for mass wasting events are in mountainous regions with relatively steep slopes. In the United States, those areas are found in the Appalachian Mountains, the Rocky Mountains, and along the Pacific Coast. However, the potential for mass wasting is not determined by slope angle alone. The highest peaks rise in western states, but the largest area at risk from landslides is in the eastern Appalachian states. Water, much more plentiful in the eastern than in the western part of the country (with the exception of the Pacific Northwest), plays a significant role in mass wasting. Other factors play other roles. Earthquakes and other natural disasters, the absence of vegetation, and human activities can also influence the potential for mass wasting.

Playing chief roles in the mass wasting process are weathering, gravity, and water.

Weathering

The process by which rocks and minerals are broken down at or near Earth's surface is called weathering. This encompasses all the processes that cause rocks and minerals to fragment, crack, crumble, or decay. There are two types of weathering: mechanical and chemical. Mechanical weathering is the process by which a rock or mineral is broken down into smaller fragments without altering its chemical makeup. Examples of this type of weathering include frost wedging, which takes place when water in a crack freezes and enlarges, forcing apart a rock. Rocks may also be forced apart in places like deserts by drastic temperature changes above freezing. The roots of trees and other plants may wedge into rocks,

Human Cost of Mass-Wasting Events

Event	Deaths	Location	Year
Loess flow	180,000	China	1920
Debris avalanche	70,000	Peru	1970
Mudflow	23,000	Columbia	1985
Debris avalanche	12,000–20,000	Soviet Union (present-day Russia)	1949
Debris avalanche	18,000	Peru	1970
Debris flow	10,000	Columbia	1999
Lahar	5,110	Indonesia	1919
Rock avalanche	4,000	Peru	1962
Rock slide	2,000	Italy	1963
Debris flow	1,000	Ecuador	1987

widening cracks. The other type of weathering, chemical weathering, is the process by which chemical reactions alter the chemical makeup of rocks and minerals. It involves the decomposition of rocks and minerals by atmospheric gases and water. Oxygen dissolved in water may oxidize minerals that contain iron. Carbon dioxide dissolved in water forms a weak carbonic acid that can dissolve limestone. Water alone may also dissolve some minerals or combine with others to form new by-products.

Rocks weather at different rates depending on the climate and their mineral composition and texture. Rocks weather rapidly in hot, moist climates, but slowly in cooler, drier climates. In general, weathering tends to produce rounded rocks. Weathering also produces regolith (pronounced REH-gah-lith). This is the layer of loose, uncemented rocks and rock fragments of various size that lies beneath the soil and above the bedrock (general term for the solid rock that underlies the soil). Over time, regolith itself can be further weathered to create soil. It is the movement of regolith downhill under the influence of gravity that defines mass wasting.

Gravity

The force of gravity acts in two ways on regolith and other material on a slope. As mentioned earlier, gravity is a constant force exerting a pull on everything on Earth's surface in a direction toward the center of the planet. Stated another way, the force of gravity pulls material straight down in a direction perpendicular to the surface. Material on a slope is thus pulled inward in a direction that is perpendicular to the slope. This helps prevent material from sliding downward. However, on a slope, gravity also exerts a force that acts to pull material down a slope, parallel to the surface of the slope. This second force of gravity is known as shear

Vehicles buried by a California mudslide that was triggered by heavy rains, 1982. **PHOTOGRAPH REPRODUCED BY PERMISSION OF THE CORBIS CORPORATION.**

stress. The amount of shear stress exerted is related directly to the steepness of the slope. Shear stress increases as the slope steepens. As shear stress increases, the perpendicular force of gravity decreases.

When shear stress becomes greater than the perpendicular force of gravity, material on a slope may still not move downward right away. It may be held in place by the frictional contact between the particles making up that material. Contact between the surfaces of the particles creates a certain amount of tension that holds the particles in place at an angle. The steepest angle at which loose material on a slope remains motionless is called the angle of repose. In general, that angle is about 35 degrees. It may vary slightly depending on certain factors, such as the size and shape of the particles. The angle of repose usually increases with increasing particle size. Particles that are irregularly shaped (with angled edges that catch on each other) also tend to have a higher angle of repose than those that have become rounded through weathering and that simply roll over each other.

Water

Water is an important agent in the process of mass wasting. Water will either help hold material together, increasing its angle of repose, or cause it to slide downward like a liquid. In mass wasting, water acts as either a glue or a lubricant. Small amounts of water can strengthen material. Slightly wet particles have a higher angle of repose because the thin film of water that exists between the particles increases the tension holding them together. An example of this action can be seen in sand. Dry sand does not stick together very well. A sand castle made of dry sand will not stand very high. Yet one made with slightly moist sand will. If too much water is added, though, the sand will become waterlogged and the castle will collapse. When material becomes saturated with water, the angle of repose is reduced to a small degree and the material tends to flow like a liquid. This occurs because the excess water completely surrounds the particles in the material, eliminating the frictional contact between the particles that holds them together.

Excess water also increases the mass of material on a slope. Mass is a measurement of how much matter is in an object, while weight is a measurement of how hard gravity is pulling on that object. The force of gravity is proportional to the mass of an object: the greater the mass, the greater the force of gravity. If the mass of the material on a slope increases, so will the force of gravity exerted on it. With low or even nonexistent frictional contact between its particles, waterlogged material is subject to high shear stress, and it will slide or flow down a slope under that force of gravity.

Triggering events

As long as material on a slope stays within its angle of repose, it will remain stationary. Good vegetative cover, a small amount of moisture, and a high amount of binding material such as clay will increase the strength and stability of a slope, preventing mass wasting. Once a slope becomes unstable, mass wasting can occur. In areas where there are alternating periods of freezing and thawing or of wetting and drying, particles of soil and regolith are lifted up and set back down, but not in the same place as before. Gravity always causes the rocks and soil to settle just a little farther downslope than from where they started. This is the slow movement that defines creep, where the slope is unstable all the time and the process is continuous.

But other times, triggering events can arise that cause a sudden instability in a slope. A sudden shock, such as shock waves from an earthquake, can alter the structure of a slope, causing the slipping of surface soil and rock and the collapse of cliffs. Volcanic eruptions produce shocks similar

A Blast of Rock

Temperature fluctuations, water freezing in cracks, and growing tree roots make rockfalls a common occurrence in Yosemite National Park in California. However, in July 1996, the ground at the park was shaken by a tremendous rockfall. An 80,000-ton (72,560-metric ton) block of granite broke free from a cliff high above Yosemite Valley near Glacier Point. It slid down a steep slope for the first 500 feet (152 meters), then took to the air and fell freely for over 1,700 feet (518 meters). The impact of the rock when it smashed into a rocky slope near the base of the cliff generated winds in excess of 160 miles (15) kilometers) per hour. The blast blew down 10 acres (4 hectares) of trees. The dust created by the impact hung in the air for several hours before settling over an area of about 50 acres (20 hectares). Places near the impact site were covered with up to 2 inches (5 centimeters) of dust.

to earthquakes. They can also cause snow and ice to melt, rapidly releasing large amounts of water that can mix with volcanic ash and regolith to produce debris flows, mudflows, and lahars. Sudden heavy rains and floods can saturate the soil and regolith, reducing frictional contact and the angle of repose.

The normal erosive action of streams and waves can undercut stream banks and cliffs along coasts. Since it is no longer at the angle of repose, the bank or cliff becomes unstable and material falls downward.

Human activities may dramatically increase mass-wasting events. Heavy trucks rumbling down a road can send shock waves through nearby unstable slopes. This is especially true in areas that have been altered by grading (leveling-off of an area) for road or building construction. When a portion of a mountainside or hillside is graded, material is cut out of the slope and removed. The slope directly above the graded area is greatly steepened, reducing support for material higher up the slope. Mining is another activity that weakens slopes and promotes mass wasting. The removal of coal, stone, and other natural resources from the area beneath a slope makes the slope unstable and vulnerable to collapse.

The removal of vegetation on a slope, such as through forest fire or the cutting down of trees, can also lead to mass wasting. The roots of trees and other plants absorb water from rain or snow and release it slowly into the soil. Roots also act as anchors, holding the soil together. Soil with no vegetative cover erodes quickly. Landslides on deforested slopes, once set in motion, have no natural barriers to slow or stop them.

Spotlight on famous forms

Frank Slide, Alberta, Canada

On April 29, 1903, in a glacier-modified valley near Alberta, Canada, the greatest landslide in recorded North American history took place. A wedge of the eastern slope of Turtle Mountain, measuring approximately 0.5 square mile (1.3 square kilometers) in area, gave way and hurtled 2,300 feet (700 meters) down the mountain. An estimated 100 million tons (91 million metric tons) of rock plowed through a portion of the nearby small coal-mining town of Frank, continued 2.5 miles (3.2 kilometers) across the valley floor, then climbed 400 feet (122 meters) up the opposite side. The fallen rock, which in places along the valley floor reached a height of 100 feet (30.5 meters), dammed the Crowsnest River and created a new lake. Seventy-six people were killed instantly in the rock slide that lasted less than two minutes. Only twelve bodies were ever recovered.

The main cause of the rock slide, which became known as the Frank Slide, was the mountain's unstable structure. Two years prior to the slide, mines had been dug in order to mine the massive deposits of coal beneath the eastern slope of the mountain. Already unstable because of the loss of rock structure underneath, the mountainside was put into further jeopardy when a sudden cold spell caused water from melting snow to freeze in cracks on its surface. As the water turned to ice, it expanded, widening the cracks and initiating the slide.

Gansu landslide, China

The Loess Plateau covers an area of about 247,100 square miles (640,000 square kilometers) in the north-central area of China. Loess (pronounced LUSS; a German word meaning "loose") is a deposit of fine, yellowish-gray, silty sediment. The loess covering the plateau was blown in from the Gobi Desert in Mongolia by windstorms over many, many years. Because it is so fine and loosely packed, loess is highly prone to erosion by wind and water.

In 1920, an earthquake struck the Loess Plateau region near Gansu (formerly Kansu) Province. Treeless and covered in loess, the hills and cliffs in the region were highly susceptible to loess flows. The shock of the earthquake caused the sides of 100-foot-high (30-meter-high) cliffs to collapse. Flowing material barricaded the entrances of mountainside caves, in which many peasants made their homes. The flows laid waste to ten cities and numerous villages in the region. An estimated 180,000 people died, more than the number who were killed at Hiroshima, Japan, on August 6, 1945, when the first atomic bomb was dropped.

Mount Huascarán debris avalanche, Peru

Mount Huascarán (pronounced wass-ka-RON), the tallest mountain in Peru, is part of the Andes mountain system, the world's longest system on land, which runs for more than 5,000 miles (8,000 kilometers) along the western coast of South America. An extinct volcano, Mount Huascarán rises to a height of 22,205 feet (6,768 meters). Like other peaks in the area, it features many alpine glaciers.

In May 1970, a forty-five-second earthquake struck beneath the mountain, causing a mass of rock and glacial ice measuring 3,000 feet (914 meters) wide and 1 mile (1.6 kilometers) long to break off its west face and slide toward the valley below. Traveling at an average speed of 100 miles (161 kilometers) per hour, the debris avalanche quickly reached the village of Yungay, located 11 miles (18 kilometers) away from the mountain. Estimated to have consisted of almost 80 million cubic yards (61 cubic meters) of rock, ice, water, and other debris, the avalanche completely buried the village and others in its path, killing 18,000 people.

Location of the Turtle Mountain landslide, which covered the town of Frank, Alberta, in 1903. **PHOTOGRAPH REPRODUCED BY PERMISSION OF THE CORBIS CORPORATION.**

For More Information

Books

Goodwin, Peter H. *Landslides, Slumps, and Creep*. New York: Franklin Watts, 1998.

Jennings, Terry. *Landslides and Avalanches*. North Mankato, MN: Thameside Press, 1999.

Walker, Jane. *Avalanches and Landslides*. New York: Gloucester Press, 1992.

Ylvisaker, Anne. *Landslides*. Bloomington, MN: Capstone Press, 2003.

Web Sites

"Avalanches and Landslides." *Nearctica*. http://www.nearctica.com/geology/avalan.htm (accessed on August 27, 2003).

"Geologic Hazards: Landslides." *U.S. Geological Survey*. http://landslides.usgs.gov/ (accessed on August 27, 2003).

"Landslide Images." *U.S. Geological Survey*. http://landslides.usgs.gov/html_files/landslides/slides/landslideimages.htm (accessed on August 27, 2003).

"Landslide Overview Map of the Conterminous United States." *U.S. Geological Survey*. http://landslides.usgs.gov/html_files/landslides/nationalmap/national.html (accessed on August 27, 2003).

"Landslides and Mass-Wasting." *Department of Geosciences, University of Arizona*. http://www.geo.arizona.edu/geo2xx/geo218/UNIT6/lecture18.html (accessed on August 27, 2003).

"Slope Failures." *Germantown Elementary School, Illinois*. http://www.germantown.k12.il.us/html/slope_failures.html (accessed on August 27, 2003).

"What Causes Landslides?" *Ministry of Energy and Mines, Government of British Columbia*. http://www.em.gov.bc.ca/mining/geolsurv/surficial/landslid/ls1.htm (accessed on August 27, 2003).

Mesa and butte

Spanish explorers in the mid-sixteenth century ranged over the American Southwest. They had come north from Mexico, looking for gold and gems and the legendary Seven Cities of Cibola (pronounced SEE-bow-lah), allegedly filled with such treasures. In their quest, they found neither gold nor riches. They did, however, become the first Europeans to view the geological wonders of the area, and they were amazed at what they saw.

Among the canyons, plateaus, and rock towers and arches, the explorers saw landforms that appeared plateaulike, only smaller and isolated. They called these geologic features mesas (pronounced MAY-suz), which means table in Spanish, because the explorers thought the landforms resembled tables with their smooth, flat tops and sides that drop away steeply. Populating the spare, arid (dry) landscape of the area along with mesas were still smaller landforms that had a similar appearance. At the beginning of the nineteenth century, the word butte (pronounced BYOOT) was coined from the French word meaning mound or hillock to describe these solitary landforms.

The shape of the land

A mesa is an isolated, flat-topped hill or mountain with steep sides that is smaller in area than a plateau. A butte is also a flat-topped hill with steep sides, though smaller in area than a mesa. Definitions of the surface areas of mesas and buttes vary. One source states that a mesa has a surface area of less than 4 square miles (10 square kilometers), while a butte has a surface area less than 11,250 square feet (1,000 square meters). Another source states that the surface area of a mesa is larger than 1 square mile (2.59 square kilometers); the surface area of a butte is smaller than that dimension. Some simply define a mesa as a

Junction Butte in Canyonlands National Park, Utah. Part of the Colorado Plateau, the landscape of sedimentary sandstone in this area was eroded into countless canyons, mesas, and buttes by the Colorado River and its tributaries. **PHOTOGRAPH REPRODUCED BY PERMISSION OF THE CORBIS CORPORATION.**

landform that is wider than it is high and a butte as one that is higher than it is wide.

A mesa's and butte's characteristic shape—flat top and clifflike sides—is due to the layers of rock forming them. These landforms are most often composed of sedimentary rock, formed by the accumulation and compression of sediment (which may consist of rock fragments, remains of microscopic organisms, and minerals). This type of rock covers more than 75 percent of Earth's land surface. Most sedimentary rocks occur in layers, called strata, that are mostly horizontal or flat when first formed. Forces within Earth that rupture the surface to form volcanoes, mountains, plateaus, and many other topographical features (physical features on the planet's surface), may later cause these layers to tip, fold, warp, or fracture.

The top layer of a mesa and a butte is a hardened layer of rock that is resistant to erosion, which is the gradual wearing away of Earth surfaces through the action of wind and water. Sometimes this top layer, called the cap rock, is not sedimentary rock but is cooled and hardened lava that had spread out across the landscape in repeated flows from fissures or cracks in

Words to Know

Canyon: A narrow, deep, rocky, and steep-walled valley carved by a swift-moving river.

Cap rock: Erosion-resistant rock that overlies other layers of less-resistant rock.

Cliff: A high, steep face of rock.

Crust: The thin, solid, outermost layer of Earth.

Erosion: The gradual wearing away of Earth surfaces through the action of wind and water.

Fault: A crack or fracture in Earth's crust along which rock on one side has moved relative to rock on the other.

Pinnacle: A tall, slender tower or spire of rock.

Plateau: A relatively level, large expanse of land that rises some 1,500 feet (457 meters) or more above its surroundings and has at least one steep side.

Plates: Large sections of Earth's lithosphere that are separated by deep fault zones.

Plate tectonics: The geologic theory that Earth's crust is composed of rigid plates that "float" toward or away from each other, either directly or indirectly, shifting continents, forming mountains and new ocean crust, and stimulating volcanic eruptions.

Sedimentary rock: Rock formed by the accumulation and compression of sediment, which may consist of rock fragments, remains of microscopic organisms, and minerals.

Strata: Layers in a series of sedimentary rocks.

the ground. Beneath this flat protective cap of rock are horizontal layers of softer sedimentary rock. To varying degrees, these layers are not as resistant to erosion.

These landforms are found in arid and semiarid regions. Arid regions are defined as those that receive less than 10 inches (25 centimeters) of rain per year; semiarid regions receive 10 to 20 inches (25 to 50 centimeters) of rain per year. Precipitation in these regions often comes in the form of sudden, heavy rainfalls. Because water evaporates quickly in these normally dry environments, plants and other ground cover are scarce. Left exposed to the action of running water, the bare sides of the softer rock layers of mesas and buttes are eroded away over time. The base of these landforms is often gently sloped, contrasting with the almost-vertical sides leading down from the top. Rock material that has been eroded from the sides is carried downward, forming this sloping base.

Forces and changes: Construction and destruction

Mesas and buttes do not arise as completed landforms through sudden geological events. They have been shaped over millions of years by the slow, orderly process of erosion. They are part of a series of landforms that naturally erode into other landforms. That series begins with plateaus, which are relatively level, large expanses of land that rise some 1,500 feet (457 meters) or more above their surroundings and have at least one steep side.

A mesa is an isolated, flat-topped hill or mountain with steep sides that is smaller in area than a plateau. A butte is also a flat-topped hill with steep sides, though smaller in area than a mesa.

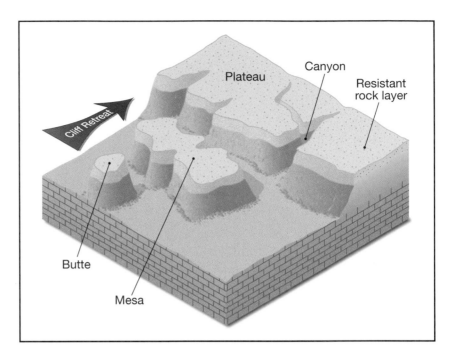

Plateaus develop in a few ways, all of which are directly related to the internal heat forces of Earth. These forces stirring beneath the crust (the outermost layer of the planet) are responsible for the physical features on the surface, from mountains to volcanoes to rift valleys and many others. Earth's internal forces have put pressure on the bottom of the crust, causing it to fracture into sections. As these sections, called plates, move about the surface in response to that pressure, they collide, slide past one another, or slide under each other. The interaction between the plates or the stress created within a plate as it has interacted with other plates have brought about the many landforms defining Earth's surface. The scientific theory explaining the plates and their movements and interactions is known as plate tectonics. (For further information on plateau formation and plate tectonics, see the **Plateau** chapter.)

Like all landforms elevated above their surrounding landscapes, a plateau is prone to erosion. Water, in the form of rain, snow, ice, rivers, runoff, and groundwater, is the primary force of that erosion. Wind also plays a part in this erosion, but to a far less degree. Rivers are the great cutting agents on plateaus. Whether raised with the plateau as it was elevated or formed afterward, a river will flow downward, seeking out the level of the body of water into which it drains. And it will do so as quickly as possible. It will seek out the path of least resistance, finding areas where rock is weak. Wearing away that rock, the river will cut downward deeper and deeper. Over millions of years, a river will form a valley, then a canyon, separating the plateau into sections. (For more information on canyon formation, see the **Canyon** chapter.)

On plateaus, areas of weak rock occur along faults, which are cracks or fractures in Earth's crust. Faults arise when pressure from underground forces pulls apart or compresses plates, creating stress within the plate. Faults are common in elevated regions. Rocks along a fault tend to be weak and broken, and a river or other flowing water easily cuts through the broken rock. Over time, valleys or canyons form, and a plateau is further dissected. (For more information on fault formation, see the **Fault** chapter.)

Rivers erode by picking up sediments (loose rock fragments) and transporting them to a new location. The speed or velocity at which a river flows determines the size of the material it can carry. A fast-moving river carries more sediment and larger material than a slow-moving one. The sediment acts as an abrasive as it is carried along, scouring and wearing away the banks and bed (sides and bottom) of the river. As new material is eroded, the river picks it up. In turn, this new sediment helps the river cut even deeper into its channel.

From plateaus to mesas to buttes to...

Geologically speaking, no landscape is ever "complete." The surface of the planet is in constant motion. As new landforms are built up, others are eroded away. As vast as it may seem, a plateau is relentlessly carved by erosion. The Colorado Plateau in the four corners region of the American Southwest is eroding at a rate of 500 vertical feet every 1 million years. Deep valleys and canyons form steep cliffs that retreat endlessly as water from storm runoff and streams and rivers washes away soft rock. Were it not for sections of resistant rock on the surface of a plateau, the entire landform would wear away over millions of years to a valley floor.

Those resistant sections allow a plateau to erode into mesas that rise above the ever-widening valley floor. Mesas maintain their shape because their cap rock offers protection to the layers of softer rock beneath. That protection, however, is short-lived. Again, water from storms washes over the sides of the mesa, wearing them away. As the sides retreat inward, the overhanging sections of cap rock weaken, fracture, and fall.

As the process of erosion continues, a mesa shrinks in size. Over time, it becomes a butte, taller than it is wide. Unrelenting, water erodes the butte as it had the mesa before it and the plateau before that. Capped by its resistant rock but ever shrinking, the butte may eventually erode into a pinnacle. This tall, slender tower or spire of rock will stand until it, too, succumbs to erosion and eventually crumbles to the valley floor.

The Face of Mars

In July 1976, the planetary probe *Viking 1* orbited Mars searching for a potential landing site for a sister probe, *Viking 2*. While photographing areas of the Cydonia region of the planet, the probe captured an image of a landform that resembled a face with darkened eyes, a narrow nose, and a frowning mouth. When the National Aeronautics and Space Administration (NASA) released the image to the public, it caused a sensation.

NASA scientists reasoned that sunlight on the landform created the apparent image, but many people thought otherwise. They believed that the face was artificially created. It was proof, they asserted, that intelligent life existed on Mars.

More than twenty years after the *Viking 1* probe was released, NASA sent another probe to Mars, the *Mars Global Surveyor*. In early 2001, after having taken tens of thousands of images of the planet, the *Surveyor* aimed its strong camera lens on the "Face of Mars." This time, the image clearly showed that the landform was simply another mesa in an area of mesas and buttes, very much like those that exist in the American Southwest.

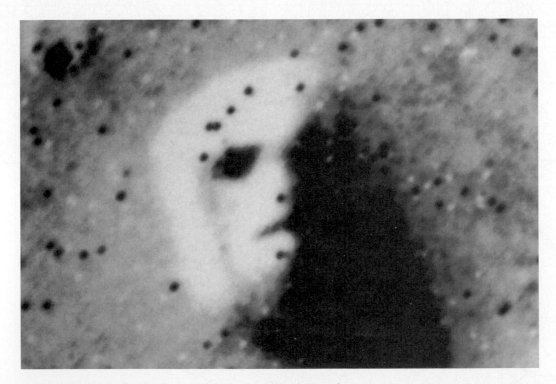

Aerial photograph of a Martian mesa that resembles a human face. **PHOTOGRAPH REPRODUCED BY PERMISSION OF THE CORBIS CORPORATION.**

Spotlight on famous forms

Enchanted Mesa, New Mexico

In west-central New Mexico stands a mesa made of sandstone, a type of rock composed of grains of sand bonded together by a mineral cement, like calcium carbonate. The mesa rises impressively 430 feet (131 meters) above the surrounding valley. Known as Enchanted Mesa, it was called Mesa Encantada by Spanish explorers and Katzimo by the Acoma (pronounced AK-ah-ma), the Native Americans who inhabit the area. The Acoma live in a pueblo (Native American village) on top of another sandstone mesa located a few miles away from Enchanted Mesa. The pueblo, believed to have been founded in the twelfth century, is the oldest continuously inhabited community in the United States.

According to Acoma legend, Enchanted Mesa is the ancestral home of the Acoma people. They lived on top of the mesa. One day, when the Acoma were tending their fields in the surrounding valley, a violent rainstorm arose. The rain washed away the stairway leading to the top of the mesa, leaving the elderly and the very young stranded on top. They eventually died from starvation. Another version of the legend states that only

The Enchanted Mesa, in Acoma Pueblo, New Mexico, rises 430 feet from the desert valley.
PHOTOGRAPH REPRODUCED BY PERMISSION OF THE CORBIS CORPORATION.

an old woman and her granddaughter were stranded on top. Rather than face certain starvation, they leapt to their deaths from the top of the mesa.

Mesa Verde, Colorado

Spanish for "green table," Mesa Verde (pronounced MAY-sah VURD or VUR-day) is a deeply carved mesa in southwest Colorado. The mesa is so-named because sagebrush, yucca, and other vegetation cover the area around it, while pinyon pine and juniper grow on its top. Unlike most mesas, the top of Mesa Verde is not completely horizontal, but tilts upward from south to north. Its north side rises nearly 2,000 feet (610 meters) above the valley below. Over millions of years, erosion has carved out the sides of the mesa. Overhangs and alcoves have developed where sections of softer sandstone layers have broken away.

Mesa Verde is perhaps more noted as a cultural landscape. Archaeologists estimate that twenty-four Native American cultures have had some connection to the area. Prominent among these were the Anasazi, who are believed to have been the ancestors of the modern Pueblo. For more than 700 years, from approximately 600 to 1300 C.E., their culture flourished at Mesa Verde. In the sheltered alcoves situated high on the mesa's sides, the Anasazi built their dwellings. Ruins of these elaborate stone structures survive to the present day. Archaeologists are not quite sure why the Anasazi abandoned their dwellings abruptly after so many centuries.

Monument Valley, Utah and Arizona

Lying entirely within the Navajo Indian Reservation on the border between southeastern Utah and northeastern Arizona is Monument Valley. Filled with striking mesas, buttes, and pinnacles, it is one of the most recognizable landscapes in the entire American Southwest. Countless Hollywood films have used the sandy region as a background, from *Stagecoach* (1939) to *Forrest Gump* (1993). More modern advertisements and television commercials are shot in Monument Valley than anywhere else on Earth.

Part of the Colorado Plateau, Monument Valley spans 2,000 square miles (5,180 square kilometers). In this flat, desolate landscape, red and orange landforms rise to heights of 1,000 feet (305 meters) or more. They are composed primarily of sandstone. Millions of years of erosion on the

---

OPPOSITE Monument Valley, a 2,000-square-mile area on the border of Utah and Arizona, is filled with mesas, buttes, and canyons. Some of the freestanding rock formations rise as high 1,000 feet from the desert floor. **PHOTOGRAPH REPRODUCED BY PERMISSION OF THE CORBIS CORPORATION.**

sedimentary rock layers of the plateau produced these isolated geological monuments.

Many of the rock formations in Monument Valley have been given names that describe their shape: East and West Mitten Buttes, Thunderbird Mesa, and Totem Pole (pinnacle), among others. The Navajo have occupied the area since the 1860s. Their history in the region, along with other Native American cultures, dates back centuries. Ancient ruins, petroglyphs (rock carvings), and pictographs (rock paintings) have been discovered throughout the area.

For More Information

Books

DenDooven, K. C. *Monument Valley: The Story Behind the Scenery*. Revised ed. Las Vegas, NV: KC Publications, 2001.

Martin, Linda. *Mesa Verde: The Story Behind the Scenery*. Revised ed. Las Vegas, NV: KC Publications, 2001.

Smith, Duane A. *Mesa Verde: Shadows of the Centuries*. Revised ed. Boulder: University Press of Colorado, 2003.

Web Sites

Butte. http://geology.about.com/library/bl/images/blbutte.htm (accessed on September 1, 2003).

"Geology of Fieldnotes: Mesa Verde National Park." *National Park Service*. http://www.aqd.nps.gov/grd/parks/meve/ (accessed on September 1, 2003).

Mesa in Sedimentary Rocks. http://geology.about.com/library/bl/images/blmesased.htm (accessed on September 1, 2003).

Mesas and Buttes. http://www.scsc.k12.ar.us/2002Outwest/NaturalHistory/Projects/WylieT/default.htm (accessed on September 1, 2003).

Meteorite crater

In July 1994, pieces of the comet Shoemaker-Levy 9 slammed into the southern hemisphere of the planet Jupiter at a speed of 37 miles (60 kilometers) per second. Professional and amateur astronomers around the world witnessed the spectacular and historic event. This marked the first time that scientists had an opportunity to witness the collision of two extraterrestrial bodies (those existing in space beyond Earth's atmosphere). Pictures taken of the impacts appeared on the Internet within hours of the event, captivating the public.

Afterward, while scientists studied data about the event, many in the public wondered if such a collision could happen to Earth and what would be the consequences. Science soon gave way to science fiction. By the end of the decade, popular movies like *Armageddon* (1998) and *Deep Impact* (1998) presented visions of Earth caught in the path of life-threatening asteroids and comets.

Although movies about planetary disasters often seem far-fetched, impacts between extraterrestrial bodies and Earth are not. In fact, an estimated 100 to 200 tons (91 to 181 metric tons) of extraterrestrial material bombards Earth's surface every day. Much of this material ranges in size from dust to pebbles and lands unnoticed. During the planet's history, though, thousands of impacts have produced craters, some of which have measured 100 miles (160 kilometers) or more in diameter. These landforms exist everywhere in our solar system except on the gaseous planets Jupiter, Saturn, Uranus, and Neptune.

The shape of the land

A meteorite is a fragment of extraterrestrial material that strikes the surface of Earth. When that material is floating in space before it hits Earth's surface, it is called a meteoroid. These terms are derived from the

Meteor Crater, also known as Barringer Crater, in Winslow, Arizona, measures nearly a mile wide and 570 feet in depth. There are more than 160 known meteorite craters on the surface of Earth. PHOTOGRAPH REPRODUCED BY PERMISSION OF PHOTO RESEARCHERS, INC.

Greek word *meteoron*, which means "phenomenon in the sky." The vast majority of meteoroids are fragments of asteroids, which are small, irregularly shaped rocky bodies that orbit the Sun. Asteroids are planetesimals (pronounced plan-ne-TESS-i-mals) or minor planets. They are ancient chunks of matter that originated with the formation of our solar system, but never came together to form a planet. The remainder of meteoroids are fragments of comets. Sometimes called "dirty snowballs," comets are clumps of rocky material, dust, frozen methane, ammonia, and water. A comet's tail, which forms as the comet approaches the Sun, is made of vaporized ice. Solar winds sweep the tail back away from the Sun.

Once a meteoroid enters Earth's atmosphere, it becomes heated due to friction and begins to glow. The glowing fragments are known as a meteor, which is more commonly known as a shooting star. A meteor that is extremely bright is called a fireball. Large swarms of meteors entering Earth's atmosphere from approximately the same direction at certain times during the year are called meteor showers.

On Earth, a meteorite crater, also known as an impact crater, forms when a meteorite greater than 3 feet (0.9 meter) in diameter hits the surface. The size and depth of the crater depend upon the size and incoming speed of the meteorite. In general, a meteorite that hits Earth's surface

Words to Know

Asteroid: A small, irregularly shaped rocky body that orbits the Sun.

Breccia: A coarse-grained rock composed of angular, broken rock fragments held together by a mineral cement.

Comet: An icy extraterrestrial object that glows when it approaches the Sun, producing a long, wispy tail that points away from the Sun.

Ejecta blanket: The circular layer of rock and dust lying immediately around a meteorite crater.

Erosion: The gradual wearing away of Earth surfaces through the action of wind and water.

Meteor: A glowing fragment of extraterrestrial material passing through Earth's atmosphere.

Meteorite: A fragment of extraterrestrial material that strikes the surface of Earth.

Meteoroid: A small solid body floating in space.

Shock wave: A wave of increased temperature and pressure formed by the sudden compression of the medium through which the wave moves.

creates a crater twelve to twenty times its size. When a meteorite slams into Earth, it forms one of two types of craters: simple or complex.

A relatively small meteorite forms a simple impact crater. Measuring typically less than 3 miles (5 kilometers) in diameter, this type of impact crater is relatively smooth, bowl-shaped, and nearly circular. The rim or upper edge of the crater is well-defined and raised above the surrounding landscape. The interior of the crater is steepest near the rim. The slope gradually decreases toward the center of the crater. Partially lining the interior of the crater is a layer of breccia (pronounced BREH-chee-ah; a coarse-grained rock composed of angular, broken rock fragments held together by a mineral cement). The energy of the impact typically causes some rocks to melt. In simple craters, this impact melt is often found as small blobs of material within the breccia layer. Surrounding the rim of the crater is a circular layer of rock and dust thrown out of the crater during its formation. Known as an ejecta blanket, this layer is deepest close to the rim. It becomes increasingly shallow outward from the crater.

A larger meteorite forms a complex impact crater, which generally measures more than 2 miles (3 kilometers) in diameter. While the interior of a complex crater may initially be smooth, it does not remain so for long. Gravity causes the steep walls to collapse downward and inward, forming terraced walls that may produce additional rims or rings within the crater. In the center of a complex crater lies a distinct central peak. The peak forms as the crater floor rebounds from the shock of the meteorite impact. The largest complex impact craters have several rings and several inner peaks. Breccia also partially fills complex craters, and its layer may contain

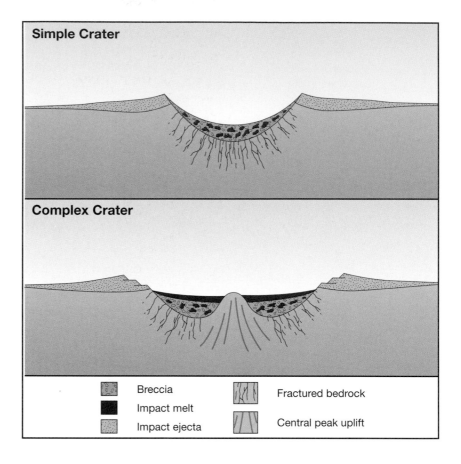

Simple Crater

Complex Crater

Breccia

Impact melt

Impact ejecta

Fractured bedrock

Central peak uplift

sheets of impact melt. An ejecta blanket surrounds a complex impact crater much as it does a simple impact crater.

Forces and changes: Construction and destruction

There are presently more than 160 known meteorite craters on the surface of Earth. Almost all have been recognized since 1950. New ones are discovered each year. The vast majority of recognized craters are found in North America, Europe, and Australia, where most exploration has taken place. Throughout the planet's history, countless other craters have existed. Like all other inner bodies in our solar system, Earth has been heavily impacted by meteorites. In fact, the planet has been impacted even more heavily than the Moon.

Yet most of these impact craters are no longer present. The geologic processes responsible for mountain building, volcanic eruptions, earthquakes, seafloor spreading, and many other physical features on the planet's surface have erased their mark. Chiefly, they have been worn

What Is a NEO?

A NEO or Near-Earth Object is an extraterrestrial body (an asteroid or a comet) whose orbit brings it within 28 million miles (45 million kilometers) of Earth's orbit. Those NEOs with orbits that actually intersect Earth's orbit are called ECOs or Earth-Crossing Objects. Scientists watch NEOs to determine which, if any, might one day strike Earth.

Any NEOs smaller than 164 feet (50 meters) in diameter would disintegrate in Earth's atmosphere. Scientists believe there are perhaps 1 million NEOs larger than this size. Although the vast majority of these measure less than 0.6 mile (1 kilometer) in diameter, they could pass through the atmosphere and cause tremendous damage if they hit the planet's surface. The largest NEOs yet discovered measure less than 15.5 miles (25 kilometers) in diameter. If one of these NEOs struck Earth, the result would be disastrous.

None of the known NEOs is currently a threat, but scientists have no way to predict the next impact from an unknown extraterrestrial object.

away by erosion, the gradual wearing away of Earth surfaces through the action of wind and water. The craters present on Earth today are either relatively recent, were caused by a relatively large meteorite, or are in a part of the world that experiences little geologic change (such as Antarctica or the Australian desert).

Scientists have never observed the formation of an impact crater in nature. They have, however, figured out the mechanics of such an event through laboratory experiments. Scientists know that an average meteoroid enters Earth's atmosphere at a velocity, or speed, between 6.2 and 43.5 miles (10 and 70 kilometers) per second. Because of friction caused by the atmosphere, all but the largest meteoroids quickly lose velocity. Most simply burn up and disintegrate before reaching Earth's surface.

Stages of impact crater formation

When a large meteorite strikes the planet's surface, enormous amounts of energy are released. Many of the characteristics of an impact crater are the result of the energy released almost instantaneously during the impact. This energy can be compared to that produced by geologic processes on Earth such as volcanic eruptions and earthquakes. The sequence of events that occurs when a meteorite strikes Earth can be divided into three stages: contact and compression, excavation, and modification.

A crater begins to form the instant a meteorite contacts Earth's surface. By the time the meteorite has penetrated the surface a distance less

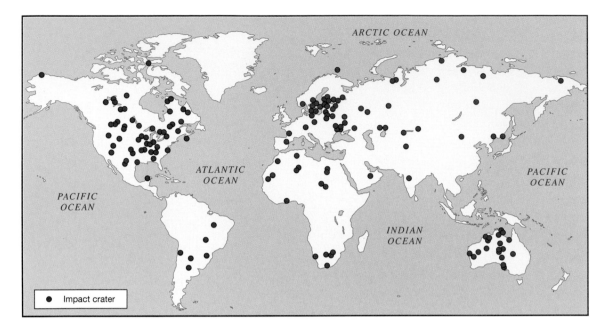

Impact crater

Map highlighting the known meteorite craters around the world.

than twice its diameter, its energy is transferred as shock waves to the rocks in the crater. (Shock waves are waves of increased temperature and pressure formed by the sudden compression of the medium through which the waves move.) Shock waves also form in the meteorite, beginning at the edge that struck the ground and moving backward. The shock waves compress the rocks in Earth's surface and the material in the meteorite. The extremely high temperature and pressure created at the area of contact melts or even vaporizes much of the rock and meteorite material in that area. As the shock waves continue to move through Earth's surface, both downward and outward, they lose speed and pressure. Rocks no longer melt, but become cracked and fractured. Rock that had been compressed in the center of the crater may rebound, forming a peak.

At almost the same time, some of the shock-wave energy forces a stream of rock and dust (the ejecta) to be thrown away from the point of impact at high speeds and in all directions. The crater takes on its characteristic bowl shape with an uplifted rim because rocks near the upper levels of the crater move upward and outward while rocks in the lower levels move downward and outward. When the ejecta settles back to the ground, it forms the ejecta blanket around the crater rim.

Finally, after the shock waves have diminished to the point where they no longer have an effect and no more material is thrown from the crater, gravity takes over. Weak rocks in the walls of the crater may fall or slide down, and portions of the ejecta may also fall back into the crater.

The crater-forming process is very rapid. The entire sequence takes anywhere from a few seconds to one minute or so. In relation to other geologic processes on Earth, impact cratering releases the greatest amount of energy in the shortest amount of time.

Despite the tremendous forces that generate meteorite craters on Earth, those craters are not permanent. Like all other landforms on the planet, they are subject to erosion and Earth's ever-shifting surface. Water and wind quickly erode crater rims and ejecta blankets. They may also fill the crater with sediments and other rock debris, forever changing its form.

Spotlight on famous forms

Chicxulub Crater, Yucatan Peninsula

Scientists believe that approximately 65 million years ago, a meteorite measuring about 6.2 miles (10 kilometers) in diameter slammed into a prehistoric ocean near present-day Mexico's Yucatan Peninsula. The buried crater is presently known as Chicxulub (pronounced cheek-soo-LOOB; from the Mayan word roughly meaning "tail of the devil"). Initially, the crater measured nearly 62 miles (100 kilometers) in diameter and 9 miles (14 kilometers) in depth. The energy released by the impact was 6 million times more powerful than that released during the 1980 eruption of Mount St. Helens in Washington state. The walls of the complex impact crater were unstable and soon collapsed inward. The final diameter of the crater was enlarged to between 90 and 112 miles (145 and 180 kilometers).

During the crater's formation, clouds of water vapor and debris were thrown into the sky. Some of the 100 billion tons (91 billion metric tons) of vaporized material solidified into glassy spheres and rained back down on Earth. The rest of the material rose into the atmosphere where winds carried it around the planet. The material blocked sunlight from reaching Earth's surface, reducing temperatures worldwide.

As the meteorite passed through Earth's atmosphere, the air friction generated searing heat, which ignited widespread wildfires. In turn, these fires produced tremendous amounts of soot, carbon dioxide, and sulfur dioxide. The sulfur dioxide reacted with moisture in the blackened air to

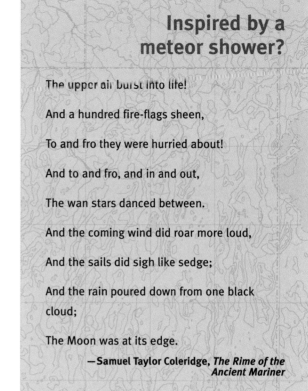

Inspired by a meteor shower?

The upper air burst into life!

And a hundred fire-flags sheen,

To and fro they were hurried about!

And to and fro, and in and out,

The wan stars danced between.

And the coming wind did roar more loud,

And the sails did sigh like sedge;

And the rain poured down from one black cloud;

The Moon was at its edge.

—Samuel Taylor Coleridge, *The Rime of the Ancient Mariner*

A Rain of Asteroids

Some 4 billion years ago, roughly the same time life was forming on the planet, a flurry of asteroids rained down on Earth and the Moon. Scientists estimate that the barrage lasted from 20 million to 200 million years. It melted rocks, blasted out craters, and reshaped the surface of both Earth and the Moon. On the Moon, the bombardment produced the great basins that are clearly visible from Earth. On Earth, the huge asteroids produced craters rim-to-rim the size of present-day continents, vaporized the oceans, and filled the atmosphere with life-choking fog. Some scientists believe the impacts may have even affected the evolution of life on the planet. The asteroids may have forced life to begin anew or may have brought minerals, water, or even the building blocks of life to Earth.

form sulfuric acid, which fell to Earth in the form of acid rain. The lack of sunlight, combined with the air pollution and acid rain, soon killed off most of the plants on the planet. This led to the starvation of many animals, both plant-eating and meat-eating. Included were the dinosaurs. It is estimated that 70 percent of all plant and animal life perished within a few months of the meteorite's impact.

Supporting the theory that this meteorite caused worldwide destruction is a layer of iridium found in Earth's crust at a depth marking that time period. Iridium is an element commonly found in meteorites, but is exceedingly rare in the planet's crust. Iridium, at thirty times the normal amount, has been found at this depth around the world, from New Zealand to Italy. Soot has also been found with the iridium, providing evidence of widespread forest fires.

Meteor Crater, Arizona

Located in the desert near Winslow, Arizona, is Meteor Crater, the first impact crater to be so recognized. The arid (dry) conditions in the area have helped preserve this classic simple impact crater. Measuring 0.8 mile (1.3 kilometers) in diameter and 570 feet (174 meters) in depth, the crater was formed roughly 50,000 years ago by a meteorite measuring 100 feet (30.5 meters) in diameter and weighing 60,000 pounds (27,240 kilograms). The rim of the crater rises 150 feet (46 meters) above the level of the surrounding desert plain. Scientists estimate that the meteorite, a solid mixture of nickel and iron, was traveling at almost 45,000 miles (72,405 kilometers) per hour when it hit Earth's surface.

Meteor Crater is also known as Barringer Crater, after Daniel Moreau Barringer (1860–1929). A mining engineer, Barringer was the first to suggest the crater was the result of a meteorite impact. Before his assertion in 1905, many geologists believed it was a volcanic crater. Barringer spent many years trying to find the iron he believed would have been left over from the meteorite. He failed to realize, however, that most of the meteorite vaporized on impact. Nonetheless, his assertion behind the crater's formation was finally, and correctly, accepted by most scientists by the 1920s.

Vredefort Crater, South Africa

The Vredefort Crater in South Africa is the world's oldest and largest recognized impact crater. Scientists believe the highly eroded complex crater formed just over 2 billion years ago when a meteorite measuring over 6.2 miles (10 kilometers) in diameter hit the area. Some 16.8 cubic miles (70 cubic kilometers) would have been vaporized in the impact. The crater, which is estimated to have measured approximately 90 by 200 miles (140 by 300 kilometers), was long thought to be of volcanic origin. It encompasses the entire extent of the present-day Witwatersrand Basin. Located within the center of the impact structure is a ring of hills called the Vredefort Dome. Measuring 43.5 miles (70 kilometers) in diameter, the ring is the eroded remains of a peak created by the rebound of rock below the impact site after the meteorite hit.

For More Information

Books

Alvarez, Walter. *T. rex and the Crater of Doom*. Princeton, NJ: Princeton University Press, 1997.

Gallant, Roy A. *Meteorite Hunter: The Search for Siberian Meteorite Craters*. New York: McGraw-Hill, 2002.

Hodge, Paul. *Meteorite Craters and Impact Structures of the Earth*. Cambridge, England: Cambridge University Press, 1994.

Mark, Kathleen. *Meteorite Craters*. Tucson: University of Arizona Press, 1987.

Steele, Duncan. *Target Earth*. Pleasantville, NY: Readers Digest, 2000.

Verschuur, Gerrit L. *Impact! The Threat of Comets and Asteroids*. Oxford, England: Oxford University Press, 1996.

Web Sites

"Asteroid and Comet Impact Hazards." *NASA Ames Research Center*. http://impact.arc.nasa.gov/index.html (accessed on September 1, 2003).

"Earth Impact Database." *Planetary and Space Centre, University of New Brunswick*. http://www.unb.ca/passc/ImpactDatabase/ (accessed on September 1, 2003).

Impact Craters. http://www.meteorite.com/impact_craters.htm (accessed on September 1, 2003).

Meteorite Central. http://www.meteoritecentral.com/ (accessed on September 1, 2003).

"Meteors, Meteorites, and Impacts." *Lunar and Planetary Laboratory, University of Arizona.* http://seds.lpl.arizona.edu/nineplanets/nineplanets/meteorites.html (accessed on September 1, 2003).

Mountain

1
2
3
4
5
6
7
8
9
10
11
12
13
14
15
16
17
18
19
20
21
22

Mountains loom large on the face of the planet. These rocky landforms, which tower over all others on Earth, are places of extreme temperatures and winds. Reaching high into the atmosphere, mountains form a barrier against moving air, robbing it of any precipitation. The tops of many mountains are laden with glossy caps of snow and ice. The summits of the highest mountains are often shrouded in mists and clouds.

Mountains also loom large in people's imaginations. Throughout human history, many people have regarded these mysterious places as the domain or home of supernatural beings or gods. Others have seen them as the ultimate in human adventure. Mountain climbing is viewed as an extreme test of human endurance and desire. Many climbers have succeeded in scaling the summits of the world's highest mountains; others have died trying.

The shape of the land

A mountain is any landmass on Earth's surface that rises abruptly to a great height in comparison to its surrounding landscape. By definition, a mountain rises 1,000 feet (305 meters) or more above its surroundings and has steep sides meeting in a summit that is much narrower in width than the mountain's base. Any highland that rises no higher than 1,000 feet (305 meters) above its surroundings, has a rounded top, and is less rugged in outline than a mountain is considered a hill. High hills at the base of mountains are known as foothills.

Mountains cover approximately one-fifth of Earth's land surface. Although rare, a mountain can exist singly, such as Mount Kilimanjaro in northeast Tanzania. Most mountains, however, occur as a group, called a mountain range. An example of a mountain range is the Sierra Nevada,

The highest mountain in the world is Mount Everest, located on the border of Tibet and Nepal. Its frozen summit stands 29,035 feet above sea level. PHOTOGRAPH REPRODUCED BY PERMISSION OF THE CORBIS CORPORATION.

which extends for about 400 miles (643 kilometers) in eastern California. A group of mountain ranges that share a common origin and form is known as a mountain system. The Sierra Madre, which arises just south of the U.S. border and extends south, is Mexico's chief mountain system. A group of mountain systems is called a mountain chain. The Pyrenees forms a mountain chain in southwest Europe between Spain and France. Finally, a complex group of mountain ranges, systems, and chains is called a mountain belt or cordillera (pronounced kor-dee-YARE-ah). The North American Cordillera runs from Alaska to Guatemala and includes all of the mountains and elevated plateaus in that vast region.

Like everything else in the natural world, mountains go though a life cycle. They rise from a variety of causes and wear down over time at various rates. The building up of mountains takes millions of years, and the process has been occurring since Earth's beginning over 4.5 billion years ago. Yet as soon as their rocks are exposed to the erosive actions of water and wind, mountains begin to fracture and dissolve. This explains the high and rugged appearance of young mountains and the lower and smoother appearance of older mountains. Some mountains that once existed on the planet hundred of millions of years ago have long since eroded away.

Words to Know

Asthenosphere: The section of the mantle immediately beneath the lithosphere that is composed of partially melted rock.

Anticline: An upward-curving (convex) fold in rock that resembles an arch.

Convection current: The circular movement of a gas or liquid between hot and cold areas.

Cordillera: A complex group of mountain ranges, systems, and chains.

Crust: The thin, solid outermost layer of Earth.

Erosion: The gradual wearing away of Earth surfaces through the action of wind and water.

Fault: A crack or fracture in Earth's crust along which rock on one side has moved relative to rock on the other.

Foothill: A high hill at the base of a mountain.

Graben: A block of Earth's crust dropped downward between faults.

Hill: A highland that rises up to 1,000 feet (305 meters) above its surroundings, has a rounded top, and is less rugged in outline than a mountain.

Horst: A block of Earth's crust forced upward between faults.

Lithosphere: The rigid uppermost section of the mantle combined with the crust.

Magma: Molten rock containing particles of mineral grains and dissolved gas that forms deep within Earth.

Magma chamber: A reservoir or cavity beneath Earth's surface containing magma that feeds a volcano.

Mantle: The thick, dense layer of rock that lies beneath Earth's crust.

Plates: Large sections of Earth's lithosphere that are separated by deep fault zones.

Plate tectonics: The geologic theory that Earth's crust is composed of rigid plates that "float" toward or away from each other, either directly or indirectly, shifting continents, forming mountains and new ocean crust, and stimulating volcanic eruptions.

Syncline: A downward-curving (concave) fold in rock that resembles a trough.

Uplift: In geology, the slow upward movement of large parts of stable areas of Earth's crust.

Orogeny (pronounced o-RAH-je-nee) is the word scientists use to describe the process of mountain building. (Orogeny comes from the Greek words *oro,* meaning "mountain," and *geneia,* meaning "born.") There are several distinct types of mountains, each having formed through varying causes: volcanic mountains, upwarped mountains, folded mountains, and fault-block mountains.

Technically, a volcano is a vent or hole in Earth's surface through which magma and other molten matter escapes from underground. Many volcanoes are classified as mountains because the magma (called lava once it reaches Earth's surface) ejected through the vent often accumulates to form a cone around the vent reaching thousands of feet in height. The shape of the accumulated landform (also known as a volcano), with a summit much narrower than its base, also fits the definition of a mountain. (For further information on volcanic landforms, see the **Volcano** chapter.)

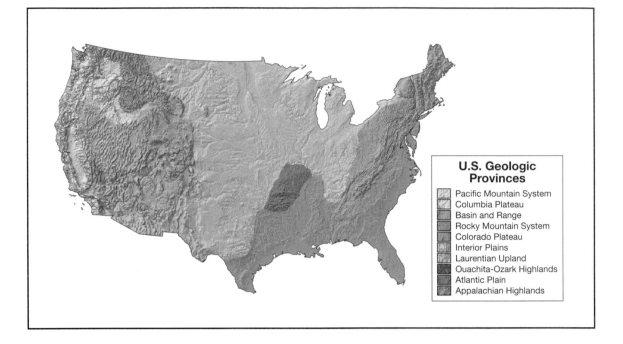

U.S. Geologic Provinces

Pacific Mountain System
Columbia Plateau
Basin and Range
Rocky Mountain System
Colorado Plateau
Interior Plains
Laurentian Upland
Ouachita-Ozark Highlands
Atlantic Plain
Appalachian Highlands

An example of a volcanic mountain in North America is Mount Rainier in the state of Washington. Part of the Cascade Range mountain chain, it rises 14,410 feet (4,392 meters) in elevation. Mauna Loa on the island of Hawaii is the world's largest volcano, rising 13,680 feet (4,170 meters) above sea level. Since it also extends more than 18,000 feet (5,544 meters) to the floor of the Pacific Ocean, Mauna Loa measures about 32,000 feet (9,754 meters) from its base to its summit. This makes it the tallest mountain on the planet (Mount Everest in the Himalayan Mountains is the tallest on land).

Most of the world's volcanic mountains lie not on land but underwater. The global mid-ocean ridge system is an undersea mountain system that snakes its way between the continents, encircling the planet like the seams on a baseball. It extends more than 40,000 miles (64,000 kilometers) in length. At the mid-ocean ridge, the seafloor splits apart and lava from below wells up into the crack or rift, solidifying and forming new seafloor. On either side of the rift lie tall volcanic mountains. The peaks of some of these mountains rise above the surface of the ocean to form islands, such as Iceland and the Azores. (For further information on oceanic landforms, see the **Ocean basin** chapter.)

Upwarped mountains are also formed by the action of rising magma. In this process, instead of passing through Earth's surface, such as it does in the formation of a volcanic mountain, magma remains underground, exerting pressure on the crust (the thin, solid outermost layer of Earth). This pressure gently uplifts a broad area of the crust, sometimes in the shape of a blisterlike dome. As the crust is uplifted, softer material on top may also be eroded or worn away by rivers or other flowing water, leaving sharp peaks and ridges. Examples of upwarped mountains in North America include the Adirondack Mountains in northeast New York and the Black Hills in western South Dakota and northeast Wyoming.

Fault-block and folded mountains are formed when stresses on Earth's crust cause it to crack and uplift or buckle and fold. As its name indicates, a fault-block mountain forms along a fault. A fault is a crack or fracture in Earth's crust along which rock on one side has moved relative to rock on the other. (For further information on faults, see the **Fault** chapter.) In the formation of a fault-block mountain, a section of the crust on one side of the fault is forced upward. The resulting mountains in the range may have steep clifflike faces on one side and gentler inclines on the other. The Teton Range of Wyoming is an example of fault-block mountains.

Folded mountains are the most common type on land. They are created when forces within Earth push adjacent sections of the crust into each other. When the sections collide, their edges along the line of collision buckle and fold in a wavelike pattern like a wrinkled rug. As the sections continue to push into each other, their leading edges are thrust higher and higher. This process has created some of the world's highest, and most famous, mountain ranges and systems. Folded mountains include those of the Appalachian Mountain system in eastern North America, the Alps mountain system in southern-central Europe, and the Himalayan mountain system in southwest Asia.

Forces and changes: Construction and destruction

Mountains form mainly as a result of movements of sections of Earth's crust in response to heat and pressure within the planet. Prior to the 1960s, geologists lacked a clear scientific explanation as to what moved continents and other sections of crust across the surface of the planet. The theory of plate

The Literary Landscape

"Straddling the top of the world, one foot in China and the other in Nepal, I cleared the ice from my oxygen mask, hunched a shoulder against the wind, and stared absently down at the vastness of Tibet. I understood on some dim, detached level that the sweep of earth beneath my feet was a spectacular sight. I'd been fantasizing about this moment, and the release of emotion that would accompany it, for many months. But now that I was finally here, actually standing on the summit of Mount Everest, I just couldn't summon the energy to care."

—Jon Krakauer, *Into Thin Air*, 1997.

Folded mountains are the most common type on land. They are created when forces within Earth push adjacent sections of the crust into each other. When the sections collide, their edges along the line of collision buckle and fold in a wavelike pattern. **PHOTO-GRAPH REPRODUCED BY PERMIS-SION OF THE CORBIS CORPORATION.**

tectonics, developed at that time, provided the answer. It explains not only how mountains are built, but also how and why volcanoes erupt, why earthquakes occur, why the seafloor spreads, and how many other topographic features (physical features on Earth's surface) are formed. Like the theory of evolution in biology, plate tectonics is the unifying concept of geology.

Earth's heated interior

At Earth's center, the inner core spins at a rate slightly faster than the planet. A blisteringly hot mass of iron, the inner core has a temperature exceeding 9,900°F (5,482°C). Around this solid inner portion is a molten, or melted, outer portion. Above the two-layered core is a large section of very dense rock called the mantle that extends upward to the crust.

The mantle itself is separated into two distinct layers: a rigid upper layer and a partially melted lower layer. The crust and the uppermost layer together make up what geologists call the lithosphere (pronounced LITH-uh-sfeer). The part of the mantle immediately beneath the lithosphere is called the asthenosphere (pronounced as-THEN-uh-sfeer). This layer is composed of partially melted rock that has the consistency of soft putty. The lithosphere is broken into many large slabs or plates that "float" on the soft asthenosphere. In constant contact with each other, these plates fit together like a jigsaw puzzle.

It is the intense heat energy created by the extreme temperatures in the core that cause the lithospheric plates to move back and forth across the surface of the planet. If this heat energy were not carried upward to Earth's surface, where it can be released in some manner, the interior of the planet would melt. This does not happen because circular currents, called convection currents, carry the energy from the core upward through the mantle.

Circulating currents

Convection takes place when material at a deeper level is heated to the point where it expands and becomes less dense (lighter) than the material above it. Once this occurs, the heated material rises. This process is similar to what happens in a pot of boiling water. As it begins to boil, water in a pot turns over and over. Heated water at the bottom of the pot rises to the surface because heating has caused it to expand and become less dense. Once at the surface, the heated water cools and becomes dense (heavier), then sinks back down to the bottom to become reheated. This continuous motion of heated material rising, cooling, and sinking within the pot forms the circular convection currents.

Convection currents form in the planet's interior when rock surrounding the core heats up. Expanding and becoming less dense, the heated rock slowly rises through cooler, denser rock that surrounds it in the mantle. When it reaches the lithosphere, the heated rock moves along the lithosphere's base, losing heat. Cooling and becoming denser, the rock then sinks back toward the core, only to be heated once again.

The pressure exerted by the convection currents underneath the lithosphere causes the plates to move. The plates, which vary in size and shape, are in constant contact with each other. When one plate moves, other plates move in response. This movement and interaction of the plates either directly or indirectly creates the major geologic features on Earth's surface, including mountains.

Plate movement and mountain building

The boundaries where plates meet and interact are known as plate margins. It is here where mountain building primarily occurs. The type of mountain that develops is dependent on the nature of the plate interaction. Plates interact by moving toward each other (converge), moving away from each other (diverge), or sliding past each other (transform). Most mountains are formed when plates converge.

When continental plates (those under the continents or landmasses) converge, the rocks in the collision area are compressed, shattered, and folded. Although normally brittle, rocks in Earth's crust can bend and fold like warm toffee when placed under great pressure and heat for long periods of time (thousands to millions of years). As the plates continue to push into each other, the rock layers are folded into a wavelike series of high points and low points. Geologists call the upfold on a curve (the peak) the anticline and the troughlike downfold (the valley) the syncline. Since tectonic plates move only a few inches per year (about as fast as fingernails grow), the process forming folded mountains takes millions of years. Folded mountains stand high because the crust beneath them is thickened as the two plates pile on each other in the collision process.

The situation is different when a continental plate and an oceanic plate converge. The crust under the oceans is made primarily of basalt, a type of rock that is denser (heavier) than the granite rocks that make up the crust under the continents. Because of this difference in density, the oceanic plate subducts or slides under the continental plate where they are pushed together. As the oceanic plate sinks deeper and deeper into Earth, intense pressure and heat in the mantle melts the leading edge of rock on the plate. This molten rock (magma) is less dense than the rock that surrounds it underground. As a result, it begins to rise toward Earth's surface through weakened layers of rock, collecting in underground reservoirs called magma chambers. When pressure from the expanding magma exceeds that of the overlying rocks, the magma is forced through cracks or vents in the planet's surface, forming volcanic mountains. Lines of volcanic mountains are usually formed on the forward edge of the continental plate.

The Andes mountain system, the world's longest system on land, runs for more than 5,000 miles (8,000 kilometers) along the western coast of South America. It features many volcanic mountains. They have formed on the edge of the continental South American Plate where the leading edge of the oceanic Nazca Plate is subducting below it. As it sinks, some crust on the top layer of the Nazca Plate is also scraped off at the base of the Andes, adding height to the system.

Volcanic mountains may also form where tectonic pressure is stretching continental crust beyond its limits. As the crust splits apart, magma rises and squeezes through the widening cracks or faults. The rising magma, whether it erupts, puts more pressure on the crust, producing

Highest Points on Land Around the World

Location	Name	Elevation
Africa (Tanzania)	Kilimanjaro	19,340 feet (5,895 meters)
Antarctica	Vinson Massif	16,860 foot (5,130 meters)
Asia (Tibet/Nepal)	Everest	29,035 feet (8,850 meters)
Australia	Kosciusko	7,316 feet (2,230 meters)
Europe, Eastern (Georgia)	Elbrus	18,481 feet (5,633 meters)
Europe, Western (France)	Mont Blanc	15,771 feet (4,870 meters)
North America (Alaska)	McKinley	20,320 feet (6,194 meters)
Oceania (New Guinea)	Jaya Peak	16,503 feet (5,030 meters)
South America (Argentina)	Aconcagua	22,835 feet (6,960 meters)

additional fractures. Ultimately, sections of the crust drop down between the faults, forming a rift valley. Volcanic mountains may then arise in or along the valley. Mount Kilimanjaro is an extinct volcano that stands along the East African Rift Valley in northeast Tanzania. It is the largest of many volcanoes in the area. Geologists believe that if the spreading of the rift valley continues, the edge of the present-day African continent will separate completely. The Indian Ocean will then flood the area, making the easternmost corner of Africa a large island.

Stress from the movement of tectonic plates can fracture continental crust. This stress or unequal pressure may be in different forms: tensional stress, which stretches or pulls rock; compressional stress, which squeezes and squashes rock; and shear stress, which changes the shape of rock by causing adjacent parts to slide past one another. When sudden stress near Earth's surface fractures brittle rock, it creates a fault in the crust.

Fault-block mountains form when tensional stress fractures the crust, separating it into blocks between faults. Pressure from magma moving underneath the surface can move the large blocks of rock (called fault blocks) either up or down. A block that is uplifted between faults is known as a horst; one that sinks is a graben (pronounced GRAH-bin). A large horst that is uplifted high between two parallel normal faults can form a fault-block mountain. More often, a fault-block mountain is created when one edge of a fault block is tilted upward at the fault a great distance in relation to the block on the other side. Sometimes these resulting landforms are referred to as tilted fault-block mountains.

Magma welling up beneath continental crust may not be able to reach Earth's surface through vents or move blocks of the crust located alongside faults. Instead, its high temperature and pressure may simply cause the overlying crust to fold and bubble gently outward into a dome shape. Over

The Black Hills stretch across 6,000 square miles of southwestern South Dakota and northeastern Wyoming. The region is home to many minerals, such as uranium and silver, and the largest gold mine in the United States is located there. PHOTOGRAPH REPRODUCED BY PERMISSION OF PHOTO RESEARCHERS, INC.

millions of years, the magma beneath the dome cools and hardens into a solid core. During the same period, erosion wears away the softer materials on top, leaving the rugged, harder material beneath exposed as an upwarped mountain.

Spotlight on famous forms

Black Hills, South Dakota and Wyoming

Some 65 million years ago, an upwelling of magma under Earth's crust in the present-day Great Plains region formed the Black Hills. These rugged mountains, which rise some 2,500 feet (760 meters), cover an area of approximately 6,000 square miles (15,540 square kilometers). The highest point in the Black Hills is Harney Peak, which stands 7,242 feet (2,207 meters) in elevation.

The Black Hills region contains large amounts of many minerals, including a few rare ones. Uranium, feldspar, mica, and silver are among the important minerals found in the area. Gold was discovered in the Black Hills in 1874. The Homestake Mine, the largest gold mine in the United States, produced more than $200 million worth of gold between 1876 and 2002.

The discovery of gold led to an invasion of white settlers into the Black Hills, forcing out local Native Americans from the area. The Lakota, Northern Cheyenne, and Omaha tribes believe the mountainous region is a sacred landscape. Two landforms the Native Americans consider particularly sacred in the Black Hills are Bear Butte and Devils Tower. Bear Butte, which rises 1,253 feet (382 meters) above the surrounding plain, is made of magma that rose, deformed the crust, then cooled and solidified. Devils Tower, standing 1,267 feet (386 meters), is a volcanic neck, the inner remains of an ancient volcano.

Cascade Range, Pacific Northwestern United States

The largest collection of volcanic mountains in the contiguous United States (connected forty-eight states) is the Cascade Range. This mountain chain extends about 700 miles (1,125 kilometers) in length. It runs south from British Columbia, Canada, through the U.S. states of Washington and Oregon before it becomes the Sierra Nevada mountain range in northeastern California. It parallels the edge of the Pacific Ocean, lying 100 to 150 miles (161 to 241 kilometers) inland from the West Coast of the United States.

The Cascade Range formed more than 30 million years ago when the oceanic Juan de Fuca Plate sunk beneath the continental North American Plate as the two plates converged. Rising magma from the leading edge of the oceanic plate created an arc of volcanic mountains. Many of these form the range's highest peaks. Mount Rainier, at 14,410 feet (4,392 meters) is the highest point in the Cascades. Other notable volcanic mountains in the range include Lassen Peak, Mount Hood, Mount Shasta, and Mount St. Helens, which last erupted in 1980. Since the Juan de Fuca Plate continues to sink beneath the North American Plate at a rate of about 1.6 inches (4 centimeters) per year, many of the volcanoes in the range are still active.

Mount Everest, on the border of Tibet and Nepal

The collision between the Indian Plate and the Eurasian Plate some 40 to 50 million years ago led to the formation of the Himalayan Mountains. The highest mountain system in the world, it features thirty mountains that rise above 25,000 feet (7,620 meters). The highest mountain in the system, and the highest on land anywhere in the world, is Mount Everest. Its frozen summit stands 29,035 feet (8,850 meters) above sea level.

Geologists estimate that when the Indian Plate moved into the Eurasian Plate, it did so at rates of up to 6 inches (15 centimeters) per year. Most plates move at rates one-fourth as fast. At present, the Indian Plate

Farthest from the Center of Earth

Although the summit of Mount Everest in the Himalayan Mountains is the highest elevation on land, it is not the farthest point from the center of Earth. That distinction goes to the volcanic mountain Chimborazo (pronounced cheem-bor-AH–so) in the Andes mountain system in central Ecuador. The highest mountain in Ecuador, Mount Chimborazo rises to a height of 20,703 feet (6,310 meters). While it is 8,832 feet (2,540 meters) lower than that of Mount Everest, its summit is actually farther away from the center of Earth because of the equatorial bulge caused by the rotation of the planet.

Earth is not a perfectly round sphere or ball; it bulges around the equator (a shape scientists call an oblate spheroid). As it revolves around the Sun, Earth also rotates or spins on its axis like a top. At the equator, the rate of this motion is slightly more than 1,000 miles (1,609 kilometers) per hour. This constant circular motion of Earth creates centrifugal force, which is the tendency of an object traveling around a central point to fly away from that point. Riders on a merry-go-round experience this same force. The centrifugal force created by Earth's rotation causes the middle of the planet to bulge slightly and the north and south poles to flatten slightly. The diameter of Earth from the North Pole to the South Pole is 7,900 miles (12,711 kilometers), but through the equator it is 7,926 miles (12,753 kilometers).

Mount Chimborazo lies very near the equator; Mount Everest lies farther north. Because of the equatorial bulge, the summit of Mount Chimborazo is 7,153 feet (2,180 meters) farther away from the center of Earth than the summit of Mount Everest.

is still inching northward, and the Himalayan Mountains are rising by as much as 0.4 inch (1 centimeter) per year.

In 1865, Mount Everest was given its English name in honor of George Everest (1790–1866), who had served as the English surveyor general of India. Tibetans call the mountain Chomolongma, meaning Mother Goddess of the World. Nepalese call it Sagarmatha, meaning Goddess of the Sky. Both hold the mountain to be sacred.

The first mountain climbers to reach the summit of Mount Everest were Edmund Hillary (1919–) of New Zealand and Tenzing Norgay (1914–1986) of Nepal on May 28, 1953. Since that time, more than 1,600 climbers have reached the summit of the world's tallest mountain. A record-breaking 54 climbers reached the peak on May 16, 2002. Not everyone who attempts to reach the top of Mount Everest is successful or even returns from the incredibly dangerous feat. The bodies of more than 160 climbers remain on the mountain.

The snow-capped peak of Mount Chimborazo stands 20,703 feet high. PHOTOGRAPH REPRODUCED BY PERMISSION OF THE CORBIS CORPORATION.

Sierra Nevadas, California

The Sierra Nevada mountain range is the largest fault-block mountain formation in the United States. It runs mainly along California's eastern border for about 400 miles (643 kilometers). Its width varies from 40 to 80 miles (64 to 129 kilometers). The highest and most rugged mountains in the range occur in its southern portion. Here, 11 peaks rise more than 14,000 feet in elevation. The summits of many of these high mountains are continuously covered with snow. The highest peak in the range, Mount Whitney, rises to 14,495 feet (4,418 meters). It is the tallest mountain in the contiguous United States (connected forty-eight states).

The blocks of crust that formed the range tilted upward along its eastern side. As a result, its eastern slope rises steeply while its western slope descends gradually to the hills in California's central valley. Forests filled with aspen, cedar, fir, pine, and sequoia trees dominate the western slope.

plateau, and it stands isolated: Over the course of several days, an individual may walk completely around the mountain at its base. Four of Asia's largest rivers also have their sources within 62 miles (100 kilometers) of the mountain. They flow away from the mountain in four different directions, like spokes from the hub of wheel: the Indus to the north, the Karnali to the south, the Yarlung Zangbo to the east, and the Sutlej to the west.

Hindus believe Mount Kailas is the dwelling place of Shiva, one of the greatest gods of Hinduism. Along with the gods Brahma and Vishnu, Shiva forms the Hindu Supreme Being. Although difficult to define simply, Hinduism is based on the concept that all living things in the universe are in a constant cycle of creation, preservation, and destruction. Shiva is the god of destruction.

Cultural Landforms

Tibetan Buddhists believe that Mount Kailas is the earthly form of mythical Mount Sumeru, the cosmic axis or center of the universe. This is the place where all planes, or realms of existence— spiritual and physical—are united.

To followers of the religions of Buddhism and Hinduism, Mount Kailas is a sacred place. Part of the Himalayan mountain system, Mount Kailas rises some 22,280 feet (6,790 meters) above the Tibetan Plateau. What is unique about the mountain is that it sits on the highest part of the

Tibetan pilgrims at the base of Mount Kailas.
PHOTOGRAPH REPRODUCED BY PERMISSION OF THE CORBIS CORPORATION.

The beauty of the Sierra Nevadas is immeasurable. Two of the nation's most-scenic national parks, Sequoia National Park and Yosemite National Park, are located within the range.

OPPOSITE The 400-mile-long Sierra Nevada mountain range, which runs along California's eastern border, was formed when the North American and Pacific plates converged many millions of years ago. Glaciers later shaped the mountains.
PHOTOGRAPH REPRODUCED BY PERMISSION OF THE CORBIS CORPORATION.

For More Information

Books

Barnes-Svarney, Patricia L. *Born of Heat and Pressure: Mountains and Metamorphic Rocks.* Berkeley Heights, NJ: Enslow Publishers, 1999.

Beckey, Fred W. *Mount McKinley: Icy Crown of North America.* Seattle, WA: Mountaineers Books, 1999.

Hill, Mary. *Geology of the Sierra Nevada.* Berkeley, CA: University of California Press, 1989.

Hubler, Clark. *America's Mountains: An Exploration of Their Origins and Influences from Alaska Range to the Appalachians.* New York: Facts on File, 1995.

Ollier, Cliff, and Colin Pain. *The Origin of Mountains.* New York: Routledge, 2000.

Rotter, Charles. *Mountains: The Towering Sentinels.* Mankato, MN: Creative Education, 2003.

Tabor, Rowland, and Ralph Taugerud. *Geology of the North Cascades: A Mountain Mosaic.* Seattle, WA: Mountaineers Books, 1999.

Wessels, Tom. *The Granite Landscape: A Natural History of America's Mountain Domes, from Acadia to Yosemite.* Woodstock, VT: Countryman Press, 2001.

Web Sites

Everest News. http://www.everestnews.com (accessed on September 1, 2003).

Geology of Rocky Mountain National Park. http://www.aqd.nps.gov/grd/parks/romo/ (accessed on September 1, 2003).

"Mountain Belts of the World." *Geosciences 20: Pennsylvania State University.* http://www.geosc.psu.edu/~engelder/geosc20/lect30.html (accessed on September 1, 2003).

"Mountain Building Learning Module." *College of Alameda Physical Geography.* http://www.members.aol.com/rhaberlin/mbmod.htm (accessed on September 1, 2003).

Mountains: An Overview. http://www.cmi.k12.il.us/~foleyma/profs/units/mountains2.htm (accessed on September 1, 2003).

Peakware World Mountain Encyclopedia. http://www.peakware.com/encyclopedia/index.htm (accessed on September 1, 2003).

Egger, Anne E. "Plate Tectonics I: The Evidence for a Geologic Revolution." *VisionLearning. http://www.visionlearning.com/library/science/geology-1/GEO1.1-plate_tectonics_1.html (accessed on September 1, 2003).*

Where to Learn More

Books

Alvarez, Walter. *T. rex and the Crater of Doom*. Princeton: Princeton University Press, 1997.

Anderson, Peter. *A Grand Canyon Journey: Tracing Time in Stone*. New York: Franklin Watts, 1997.

Aulenbach, Nancy Holler, and Hazel A. Barton. *Exploring Caves: Journeys into the Earth*. Washington, D.C.: National Geographic, 2001.

Baars, Donald L. *A Traveler's Guide to the Geology of the Colorado Plateau*. Salt Lake City: University of Utah Press, 2002.

Barnes, F. A. *Canyon Country Geology*. Thompson Springs, UT: Arch Hunter Books, 2000.

Barnes-Svarney, Patricia L. *Born of Heat and Pressure: Mountains and Metamorphic Rocks*. Berkeley Heights, NJ: Enslow Publishers, 1999.

Beckey, Fred. *Mount McKinley: Icy Crown of North America*. Seattle, WA: Mountaineers Books, 1999.

Benn, Douglas I., and David J. A. Evans. *Glaciers and Glaciation*. London, England: Edward Arnold, 1998.

Bennett, Matthew R., and Neil F. Glasser. *Glacial Geology: Ice Sheets and Landforms*. New York: John Wiley and Sons, 1996.

Bird, Eric. *Coastal Geomorphology: An Introduction*. New York: John Wiley and Sons, 2000.

Bowen, James, and Margarita Bowen. *The Great Barrier Reef: History, Science, Heritage*. New York: Cambridge University Press, 2002.

Bridge, John S. *Rivers and Floodplains: Forms, Processes, and Sedimentary Record*. Malden, MA: Blackwell, 2002.

Brimner, Larry Dane. *Geysers*. New York: Children's Press, 2000.

Bryan, T. Scott. *The Geysers of Yellowstone*. Third ed. Boulder: University Press of Colorado, 1995.

Cerullo, Mary M. *Coral Reef: A City That Never Sleeps*. New York: Cobblehill, 1996.

Collard, Sneed B. *Lizard Island: Science and Scientists on Australia's Great Barrier Reef*. New York: Franklin Watts, 2000.

Collier, Michael. *A Land in Motion: California's San Andreas Fault*. Berkeley: University of California Press, 1999.

Davis, Richard A., Jr. *The Evolving Coast*. New York: W. H. Freeman, 1997.

Decker, Robert, and Barbara Decker. *Volcanoes*. New York: W. H. Freeman, 1997.

DenDooven, K. C. *Monument Valley: The Story Behind the Scenery*. Revised ed. Las Vegas, NV: KC Publications, 2001.

Downs, Sandra. *Earth's Fiery Fury*. Brookfield, CT: Twenty-First Century Books, 2000.

Erickson, Jon. *Glacial Geology: How Ice Shapes the Land*. New York: Facts on File, 1996.

Erickson, Jon. *Marine Geology: Exploring the New Frontiers of the Ocean*. Revised ed. New York: Facts on File, 2002.

Fisher, Richard D. *Earth's Mystical Grand Canyons*. Tucson, AZ: Sunracer Publications, 2001.

Gallant, Roy A. *Geysers: When Earth Roars*. New York: Scholastic Library Publishing, 1997.

Gallant, Roy A. *Meteorite Hunter: The Search for Siberian Meteorite Craters*. New York: McGraw-Hill, 2002.

Gallant, Roy A. *Sand on the Move: The Story of Dunes*. New York: Franklin Watts, 1997.

Gillieson, David S. *Caves: Processes, Development, and Management*. Cambridge, MA: Blackwell Publishers, 1996.

Goodwin, Peter H. *Landslides, Slumps, and Creep*. New York: Franklin Watts, 1998.

Harden, Deborah R. *California Geology*. Englewood Cliffs, NJ: Prentice Hall, 1997.

Haslett, Simon. *Coastal Systems*. New York: Routledge, 2001.

Hecht, Jeff. *Shifting Shores: Rising Seas, Retreating Coastlines*. New York: Atheneum, 1990.

Hill, Mary. *Geology of the Sierra Nevada*. Berkeley: University of California Press, 1989.

Hodge, Paul. *Meteorite Craters and Impact Structures of the Earth*. Cambridge, England: Cambridge University Press, 1994.

Hook, Cheryl. *Coral Reefs*. Philadelphia, PA: Chelsea House, 2001.

Huber, N. King. *The Geologic Story of Yosemite National Park*. Washington, D.C.: U.S. Geological Survey, 1987.

Hubler, Clark. *America's Mountains: An Exploration of Their Origins and Influences from Alaska Range to the Appalachians*. New York: Facts on File, 1995.

Jennings, Terry. *Landslides and Avalanches*. North Mankato, MN: Thameside Press, 1999.

Knox, Ray, and David Stewart. *The New Madrid Fault Finders Guide*. Marble Hill, MO: Gutenberg-Richter Publications, 1995.

Ladd, Gary. *Landforms, Heart of the Colorado Plateau: The Story Behind the Scenery*. Las Vegas, NV: KC Publications, 2001.

Lancaster, Nicholas. *The Geomorphology of Desert Dunes*. New York: Routledge, 1995.

Leopold, Luna B. *A View of the River*. Cambridge, MA: Harvard University Press, 1994.

Leopold, Luna B. *Water, Rivers and Creeks*. Sausalito, CA: University Science Books, 1997.

Llewellyn, Claire. *Glaciers*. Barrington, IL: Heinemann Library, 2000.

Mark, Kathleen. *Meteorite Craters*. Tucson: University of Arizona Press, 1987.

Martin, Linda. *Mesa Verde: The Story Behind the Scenery*. Revised ed. Las Vegas, NV: KC Publications, 2001.

Martin, Patricia A. Fink. *Rivers and Streams*. New York: Franklin Watts, 1999.

Massa, Renato. *The Coral Reef*. Translated by Linda Serio. Austin, TX: Raintree Steck-Vaughn, 1998.

McPhee, John. *Basin and Range*. New York: Farrar, Strauss, and Giroux, 1981.

Moore, George W., and Nicholas Sullivan. *Speleology: Caves and the Cave Environment*. Third ed. St. Louis, MO: Cave Books, 1997.

Morris, Neil. *Volcanoes*. New York: Crabtree Publishing, 1995.

Ollier, Cliff, and Colin Pain. *The Origin of Mountains*. New York: Routledge, 2000.

Palmer, Arthur N., and Kathleen H. Lavoie. *Introduction to Speleology*. St. Louis, MO: Cave Books, 1999.

Post, Austin, and Edward R. Lachapelle. *Glacier Ice*. Revised ed. Seattle: University of Washington Press, 2000.

Price, L. Greer. *An Introduction to Grand Canyon Geology*. Grand Canyon, AZ: Grand Canyon Association, 1999.

Rosi, Mauro, Papale, Paolo, Lupi, Luca, and Marco Stoppato. *Volcanoes*. Toronto: Firefly Books, 2003.

Rotter, Charles. *Mountains: The Towering Sentinels*. Mankato, MN: Creative Education, 2003.

Schuh, Mari C. *What Are Rivers?* Mankato, MN: Pebble Books, 2002.

Seibold, E., and W. H. Berger. *The Sea Floor*. Third ed. New York: Springer Verlag, 1996.

Sheppard, Charles. *Coral Reefs: Ecology, Threats, and Conservation*. Stillwater, MN: Voyageur Press, 2002.

Smith, Duane A. *Mesa Verde: Shadows of the Centuries*. Revised ed. Boulder: University Press of Colorado, 2003.

Steele, Duncan. *Target Earth*. Pleasantville, NY: Reader's Digest, 2000.

Tabor, Rowland, and Ralph Taugerud. *Geology of the North Cascades: A Mountain Mosaic*. Seattle, WA: Mountaineers Books, 1999.

Taylor, Michael Ray. *Caves: Exploring Hidden Realms*. Washington, D.C.: National Geographic, 2001.

Thompson, Luke. *Volcanoes*. New York: Children's Press, 2000.

Tilling, Robert I. *Born of Fire: Volcanoes and Igneous Rocks*. Berkeley Heights, NJ: Enslow, 1991.

Trimble, Stephen. *The Sagebrush Ocean: A Natural History of the Great Basin*. Reno: University of Nevada Press, 1999.

Trueit, Trudy Strain. *Volcanoes*. New York: Franklin Watts, 2003.

Vallier, Tracy. *Islands and Rapids: The Geologic Story of Hells Canyon*. Lewiston, ID: Confluence Press, 1998.

Van Rose, Susanna. *Volcano and Earthquake*. New York: DK Publishing, 2000.

Verschuur, Gerrit L. *Impact! The Threat of Comets and Asteroids*. Oxford, England: Oxford University Press, 1996.

Walker, Jane. *Avalanches and Landslides*. New York: Gloucester Press, 1992.

Wessels, Tom. *The Granite Landscape: A Natural History of America's Mountain Domes, from Acadia to Yosemite*. Woodstock, VT: Countryman Press, 2001.

Williams, David B. *A Naturalist's Guide to Canyon Country*. Helena, MT: Falcon Publishing Company, 2001.

Ylvisaker, Anne. *Landslides*. Bloomington, MN: Capstone Press, 2003.

Web sites

"About Coral Reefs." *U.S. Environmental Protection Agency*. http://www.epa.gov/owow/oceans/coral/about.html (accessed on August 14, 2003).

"All About Glaciers." *National Snow and Ice Data Center*. http://nsidc.org/glaciers/ (accessed on September 1, 2003).

"Asteroid and Comet Impact Hazards." *NASA Ames Research Center*. http://impact.arc.nasa.gov/index.html (accessed on September 1, 2003).

"Atlantic Plain Province." *U.S. Geological Survey and the National Park Service*. http://wrgis.wr.usgs.gov/docs/parks/province/atlantpl.html (accessed on August 6, 2003).

"Avalanches and Landslides." *Nearctica*. http://www.nearctica.com/geology/avalan.htm (accessed on August 27, 2003).

"Basics of Flooding." *Floodplain Management Association*. http://www.floodplain.org/flood_basics.htm (accessed on September 1, 2003).

"Basin and Coastal Morphology: Principal Features." *COAST Resource Guide*. http://www.coast-nopp.org/visualization_modules/physical_chemical/basin_coastal_morphology/principal_features/index.html (accessed on September 23, 2003).

Butte. http://geology.about.com/library/bl/images/blbutte.htm (accessed on September 1, 2003).

"Cascades Volcano Observatory: Learn About Volcanoes." *U.S. Geological Survey*. http://vulcan.wr.usgs.gov/Outreach/AboutVolcanoes/framework.html (accessed on September 2, 2003).

"Cave Facts." *American Cave Conservation Association*. http://www.cavern.org/CAVE/ACCA_index.htm (accessed on August 14, 2003).

"Caves Theme Page." *Gander Academy*. http://www.stemnet.nf.ca/CITE/cave.htm (accessed on August 14, 2003).

"Coastal and Marine Geology Program." *U.S. Geological Survey*. http://marine.usgs.gov/index.html (accessed on August 14, 2003).

Coastal Processes and the Continental Margins. http://www.ocean.washington.edu/education/magic/Ipage/happened/2/coastal.htm (accessed on September 23, 2003).

"The Coastal Scene: Oceanography from the Space Shuttle." *Goddard Space Flight Center, National Aeronautics and Space Administration.* http://daac.gsfc.nasa.gov/CAMPAIGN_DOCS/OCDST/shuttle_oceanography_web/oss_4.html (accessed on August 14, 2003).

"The Colorado Plateau: High, Wide, & Windswept." *BLM Environmental Education.* http://www.blm.gov/education/colplateau/index.html (accessed on September 2, 2003).

"Colorado Plateau Province." *U.S. Geological Survey.* http://wrgis.wr.usgs.gov/docs/parks/province/coloplat.html (accessed on August 14, 2003).

"Coral Reef Ecosystems: Tropical Rain Forest of the Sea." *Department of Geology, San Jose State University.* http://geosun1.sjsu.edu/~dreed/105/coral.html (accessed on August 14, 2003).

Coral reefs. http://www.starfish.ch/reef/reef.html (accessed on August 14, 2003).

"Coral Reefs and Associated Ecosystems." *National Oceanographic Data Center, National Oceanic and Atmospheric Administration.* http://www.nodc.noaa.gov/col/projects/coral/Coralhome.html (accessed on August 14, 2003).

"Deep Ocean Basins." *COAST Resource Guide.* http://www.coast-nopp.org/visualization_modules/physical_chemical/basin_coastal_morphology/principal_features/deep_ocean/basins.html (accessed on August 4, 2003).

"Delta." *Kent National Grid for Learning.* http://www.kented.org.uk/ngfl/rivers/River%20Articles/delta.htm (accessed on August 26, 2003).

"Deltas." *Department of Geological Sciences, Salem State College.* http://www.salem.mass.edu/~lhanson/gls214/gls214_deltas.html (accessed on August 26, 2003).

"Desert Geologic Features." *Desert USA.* http://www.desertusa.com/mag99/sep/papr/desfeatures.html (accessed on August 26, 2002).

"Deserts: Geology and Resources." *U.S. Geological Survey.* http://pubs.usgs.gov/gip/deserts/ (accessed on August 26, 2002).

"Earth Impact Database." *Planetary and Space Science Centre, University of New Brunswick.* http://www.unb.ca/passc/ImpactDatabase/ (accessed on September 1, 2003).

"Earth's Water: River and Streams." *U.S. Geological Survey.* http://ga.water.usgs.gov/edu/earthrivers.html (accessed on August 14, 2003).

Egger, Anne E. "Plate Tectonics I: The Evidence for a Geologic Revolution." *VisionLearning*. http://www.visionlearning.com/library/science/geology-1/GEO1.1-plate_tectonics_1.html (accessed on September 1, 2003).

The Electronic Volcano. http://www.dartmouth.edu/~volcano/ (accessed on September 2, 2003).

EOSC 110: Desert Photos. http://www.eos.ubc.ca/courses/eosc110/fletcher/slideshow/deserts/deserts.html (accessed on August 26, 2002).

Everest News. http://www.everestnews.com (accessed on September 1, 2003).

"Explore the Geological Wonders of South Africa—Visit the Geology of the Witwatersrand." *Geological Heritage Tours*. http://www.geosites.co.za/witsgeology.htm (accessed on August 14, 2003).

"Fault Motion." *Incorporated Research Institutions for Seismology*. http://www.iris.edu/gifs/animations/faults.htm (accessed on September 1, 2003).

"Floodplain Features and Management." *Shippensburg University*. http://www.ship.edu/~cjwolt/geology/fpl.htm (accessed on September 1, 2003).

"Floods and Flood Plains." *U.S. Geological Survey*. http://water.usgs.gov/pubs/of/ofr93-641/ (accessed on September 1, 2003).

"Ganges River Delta (image)." *Earth Observatory, NASA*. http://earthobservatory.nasa.gov/Newsroom/NewImages/images.php3?img_id=4793 (accessed on August 26, 2003).

"Geologic Hazards: Landslides." *U.S. Geological Survey*. http://landslides.usgs.gov/ (accessed on August 27, 2003).

"Geology of Fieldnotes: Mesa Verde National Park." *National Park Service*. http://www.aqd.nps.gov/grd/parks/meve/ (accessed on September 1, 2003).

Geology of Great Basin National Park. http://www.aqd.nps.gov/grd/parks/grba/ (accessed on August 14, 2003).

Geology of Rocky Mountain National Park. http://www.aqd.nps.gov/grd/parks/romo/ (accessed on September 1, 2003).

"The Geology of the Grand Canyon." *Grand Canyon Explorer*. http://www.kaibab.org/geology/gc_geol.htm (accessed on August 14, 2003).

Geology of Tibet Plateau, the Roof of the World. http://www.100gogo. com/geo.htm (accessed on September 2, 2003).

Geomorphology of the Sonoran Desert. http://alic.arid.arizona.edu/sonoran/ Physical/geomorphology.html (accessed on August 26, 2002).

"Geothermal Energy and Hydrothermal Activity: Fumaroles, Hot Springs, Geysers." *U.S. Geological Survey.* http://vulcan.wr.usgs.gov/ Glossary/ThermalActivity/description_thermal_activity.html (accessed on September 1, 2003).

The Geyser Observation and Study Association. http://www.geyserstudy.org/ (accessed on September 1, 2003).

"Geysers, Fumaroles, and Hot Springs." *U.S. Geological Survey.* http://pubs.usgs.gov/gip/volc/geysers.html (accessed on September 1, 2003).

"Glacial Landforms." *South Central Service Cooperative.* http://www.scsc. k12.ar.us/2001Outwest/PacificEcology/Projects/HendricksR/default.htm (accessed on September 1, 2003).

"A Glacier Carves a U-Shaped Valley." *U.S. Geological Survey and the National Park Service.* http://wrgis.wr.usgs.gov/docs/parks/glacier/ uvalley.html (accessed on August 14, 2003).

"Glaciers and Glacial Geology." *Montana State University-Bozeman.* http://gemini.oscs.montana.edu/~geol445/hyperglac/index.htm (accessed on September 1, 2003).

Glaciers, Rivers of Ice. http://members.aol.com/scipioiv/glmain.html (accessed on September 1, 2003).

"Global Volcanism Program." *Smithsonian Institution.* http://www.volcano. si.edu/gvp/ (accessed on September 2, 2003).

"Grand Canyon National Park: Geologic Story." *National Park Service.* http://www.nps.gov/grca/grandcanyon/quicklook/Geologicstory.htm (accessed on August 14, 2003).

"The Great Artesian Basin Information Site." *The State of Queensland Department of Natural Resources and Mines.* http://www.nrm.qld.gov. au/water/gab/ (accessed on August 14, 2003).

"The Great Plains and Prairies." *U.S. Department of State.* http://usinfo. state.gov/products/pubs/geography/geog11.htm (accessed on August 6, 2003).

"Harry Hammond Hess: Spreading the Seafloor." *U.S. Geological Survey.* http://pubs.usgs.gov/publications/text/HHH.html (accessed on August 4, 2003).

"Hayward Fault." *The Berkeley Seismological Laboratory.* http://www.seismo.berkeley.edu/seismo/hayward/ (accessed on September 1, 2003).

"Illustrated Glossary of Alpine Glacial Landforms." *Department of Geography and Geology, University of Wisconsin-Stevens Point.* http://www.uwsp.edu/geo/faculty/lemke/alpine_glacial_glossary/glossary.html (accessed on September 1, 2003).

Impact Craters. http://www.meteorite.com/impact_craters.htm (accessed on September 1, 2003).

"Infrared Yellowstone Gallery." *Infrared Processing and Analysis Center, California Institute of Technology.* http://coolcosmos.ipac.caltech.edu/image_galleries/ir_yellowstone/ (accessed on September 1, 2003).

"Interior Plains Province." *U.S. Geological Survey and the National Park Service.* http://wrgis.wr.usgs.gov/docs/parks/province/intplain.html (accessed on August 6, 2003).

"Karst Topography Teacher's Guide and Paper Model." *U.S. Geological Survey.* http://wrgis.wr.usgs.gov/docs/parks/cave/karst.html (accessed on August 14, 2003).

"Landslide Images." *U.S. Geological Survey.* http://landslides.usgs.gov/html_files/landslides/slides/landslideimages.htm (accessed on August 27, 2003).

"Landslide Overview Map of the Conterminous United States." *U.S. Geological Survey.* http://landslides.usgs.gov/html_files/landslides/nationalmap/national.html (accessed on August 27, 2003).

"Landslides and Mass-Wasting." *Department of Geosciences, University of Arizona.* http://www.geo.arizona.edu/geo2xx/geo218/UNIT6/lecture18.html (accessed on August 27, 2003).

"Lava Plateaus and Flood Basalts." *U.S. Geological Survey.* http://vulcan.wr.usgs.gov/Glossary/LavaPlateaus/description_lava_plateaus.html (accessed on September 2, 2003).

"Major Deltas of the World." *Department of Geology and Geophysics, University of Wyoming.* http://faculty.gg.uwyo.edu/heller/Sed%20Strat%20Class/Sedstrat6/slideshow_6_1.htm (accessed on August 26, 2003).

Mesa in Sedimentary Rocks. http://geology.about.com/library/bl/images/blmesased.htm (accessed on September 1, 2003).

Mesas and Buttes. http://www.scsc.k12.ar.us/2002Outwest/NaturalHistory/Projects/WylieT/default.htm (accessed on September 1, 2003).

Meteorite Central. http://www.meteoritecentral.com/ (accessed on September 1, 2003).

"Meteors, Meteorites, and Impacts." *Lunar and Planetary Laboratory, University of Arizona.* http://seds.lpl.arizona.edu/nineplanets/nineplanets/meteorites.html (accessed on September 1, 2003).

"Mid-Ocean Ridge." *Woods Hole Oceanographic Institute*. http://www. divediscover.whoi.edu/infomods/midocean/ (accessed on August 4, 2003).

"Mississippi River Delta (image)." *Earth Observatory, NASA*. http://earthobservatory.nasa.gov/Newsroom/NewImages/images.php3 ?img_id=9304 (accessed on August 26, 2003).

"Mountain Belts of the World." *Geosciences 20: Pennsylvania State University*. http://www.geosc.psu.edu/~engelder/geosc20/lect30.html (accessed on September 1, 2003).

"Mountain Building Learning Module." *College of Alameda Physical Geography*. http://www.members.aol.com/rhaberlin/mbmod.htm (accessed on September 1, 2003).

Mountains: An Overview. http://www.cmi.k12.il.us/~foleyma/profs/ units/mountains2.htm (accessed on September 1, 2003).

Mustoe, M. *Every Place Has Its Faults!* http://www.tinynet.com/faults. html (accessed on September 1, 2003).

"The New Madrid Fault Zone." *The Arkansas Center for Earthquake Education and Technology Transfer*. http://quake.ualr.edu/public/nmfz.htm (accessed on September 1, 2003).

"NOVA: Mysterious Life of Caves." *WGBH Educational Foundation*. http://www.pbs.org/wgbh/nova/caves/ (accessed on August 14, 2003).

"Ocean Regions: Ocean Floor-Characteristics." *Office of Naval Research*. http://www.onr.navy.mil/focus/ocean/regions/oceanfloor1.htm (accessed on August 4, 2003).

"Ocean Regions: Ocean Floor-Continental Margin and Rise." *Office of Naval Research*. http://www.onr.navy.mil/focus/ocean/regions/ oceanfloor2.htm (accessed on September 23, 2003).

"Okavango Delta and Makgadikgadi Pans, Botswana (image)." *Visible Earth, NASA*. http://visibleearth.nasa.gov/cgi-bin/viewrecord?9152 (accessed on August 26, 2003).

Park Geology Tour: Colorado Plateau. http://www2.nature.nps.gov/grd/ tour/cplateau.htm (accessed on September 2, 2003).

"Park Geology Tour of Cave and Karst Parks." *National Park Service, Geologic Resources Division*. http://www.aqd.nps.gov/grd/tour/ caves.htm (accessed on August 14, 2003).

Park Geology Tour of Sand Dune Parks. http://www.aqd.nps.gov/grd/tour/ sanddune.htm (accessed on August 26, 2002).

"Park Geology Tour of Shoreline Geology." *National Park Service, Geologic Resources Division*. http://www2.nature.nps.gov/grd/tour/ coastal.htm (accessed on August 14, 2003).

Peakware World Mountain Encyclopedia. http://www.peakware.com/ encyclopedia/index.htm (accessed on September 1, 2003).

Plate Tectonics. http://www.platetectonics.com/ (accessed on August 14, 2003).

"ReefBase: A Global Information System on Coral Reefs." *WorldFish Center,* http://www.reefbase.org/ (accessed on August 14, 2003).

RiverResource. http://riverresource.com/ (accessed on August 14, 2003).

"Rivers and Streams." *Missouri Botanical Garden.* http://mbgnet.mobot. org/fresh/rivers/index.htm (accessed on August 14, 2003).

"River World." *Kent National Grid for Learning.* http://www.kented. org.uk/ngfl/rivers/index.html (accessed on August 14, 2003).

"Sand Dunes." *Desert USA.* http://www.desertusa.com/geofacts/ sanddune.html (accessed on August 26, 2002).

Schultz, Sandra S., and Robert E. Wallace. "The San Andreas Fault." *U.S. Geological Survey.* http://pubs.usgs.gov/gip/earthq3/ safaultgip.html (accessed on September 1, 2003).

"The Sea Floor Spread." *Public Broadcasting Service.* http://www.pbs.org/ wgbh/aso/tryit/tectonics/divergent.html (accessed on August 4, 2003).

"Slope Failures." *Germantown Elementary School, Illinois.* http://www. germantown.k12.il.us/html/slope_failures.html (accessed on August 27, 2003).

"Slot Canyons of the American Southwest." *The American Southwest.* http://www.americansouthwest.net/slot_canyons/index.html (accessed on August 14, 2003).

"This Dynamic Earth: The Story of Plate Tectonics." *U.S. Geological Survey.* http://pubs.usgs.gov/publications/text/dynamic.html (accessed on August 4, 2003).

Tilling, Robert I. "Volcanoes." *U.S. Geological Survey.* http://pubs.usgs. gov/gip/volc/ (accessed on September 2, 2003).

Trimble, Donald E. "The Geologic Story of the Great Plains." *North Dakota State University Libraries.* http://www.lib.ndsu.nodak.edu/ govdocs/text/greatplains/text.html (accessed on August 6, 2003).

United States Coral Reef Task Force. http://coralreef.gov/ (accessed on August 14, 2003).

"Valley and Stream Erosion." *Bryant Watershed Project.* http://www. watersheds.org/earth/valley.htm (accessed on August 14, 2003).

Valley Glaciers. http://www.zephryus.demon.co.uk/geography/resources/glaciers/ valley.html (accessed on August 14, 2003).

"Virtual River." *Geology Labs On-line Project*. http://vcourseware. sonoma.edu/VirtualRiver/ (accessed on August 14, 2003).

Volcanic Landforms. http://volcano.und.nodak.edu/vwdocs/vwlessons/ landforms.html (accessed on September 2, 2003).

Volcanic Landforms of Hawaii Volcanoes National Park. http://volcano. und.nodak.edu/vwdocs/vwlessons/havo.html (accessed on September 2, 2003).

Volcano World. http://volcano.und.nodak.edu/ (accessed on September 2, 2003).

"Volcanoes of the United States." *U.S. Geological Survey*. http://pubs. usgs.gov/gip/volcus/ (accessed on September 2, 2003).

Wassman, Cliff. *Mysterious Places: Hidden Slot Canyons*. http://www. mysteriousplaces.com/HiddnCany.html (accessed on August 14, 2003).

"What Causes Landslides?" *Ministry of Energy and Mines, Government of British Columbia*. http://www.em.gov.bc.ca/mining/geolsurv/ surficial/landslid/ls1.htm (accessed on August 27, 2003).

"When Rivers Run Into the Ocean." *Missouri Botanical Garden*. http://mbgnet.mobot.org/fresh/rivers/delta.htm (accessed on August 26, 2003).

"Where Parks Meet the Sea." *U.S. Geological Survey and the National Park Service*. http://www2.nature.nps.gov/grd/usgsnps/sea/sea.html (accessed on August 14, 2003).

"World Geyser Fields." *Department of Geography and Geology, Western Kentucky University*. http://www.uweb.ucsb.edu/~glennon/geysers/ (accessed on September 1, 2003).

"World Ocean Floors." *Platetectonics.com*. http://www.platetectonics.com/ oceanfloors/index.asp (accessed on August 4, 2003).

WyoJones' Geyser Site. http://www.web-net.com/jonesy/geysers.htm (accessed on September 1, 2003).

Index

Italic type indicates volume number; (ill.) indicates photos and illustrations.

A

Aa 3: 294

Ablation zone 2: 160, 165 (ill.), 166

Abyssal plain 1: 65 (ill.), 3: 227, 228, 243, 244

Accretionary wedge 1: 59, 65 (ill.)

Accumulation zone 2: 160, 166

Acoma 2: 193, 194

Active continental margin 1: 59, 60, 65 (ill.), 66

African Plate 2: 125 (ill.), 3: 303 (ill.)

Alaska 2: 125–127, 126 (ill.), 215

Alberta, Canada 2: 184, 185 (ill.)

Algodones Sand Dunes, California 1: 108–110, 109 (ill.)

Alluvial fan 1: 60, 84, 85, 95, 97, 99, 108, 3: 243, 265, 267, 271

Alluvium 1: 83, 85, 2: 133–136, 3: 243, 266, 267, 274

Alpine glacier 2: 160, 161, 162, 164, 167, 169, 185, 3: 281, 282

Amazon River 3: 275, 275 (ill.)

Anasazi 1: 26, 27 (ill.), 2: 194

Andes Mountains 1: 66, 2: 185, 214, 218, 3: 237, 275, 308

Angel Falls, Venezuela 3: 270

Angle of repose 2: 176, 181–183

Antarctic Plate 2: 125 (ill.), 3: 303 (ill.)

Antarctica 1: 60, 62, 2: 160, 168, 169, 201, 215, 3: 251, 255, 282

Antelope Canyon, Arizona 1: 23, 24 (ill.)

Anticline 1: 5–7, 6 (ill.), 2: 209, 214

Appalachian Highlands 2: 210 (ill.)

Arabian Plate 2: 125 (ill.), 3: 303 (ill.)

Archipelago 1: 79, 79 (ill.)

Arcuate delta 1: 85–86

Arête 2: 160, 162, 163 (ill.), 169–170

Argentina 2: 215, 3: 269 (ill.), 276, 276 (ill.)

Arizona 1: 23, 25–26, 2: 194, 195 (ill.), 198 (ill.), 204–205

Arkansas 2: 154–155

Armageddon 2: 197

Arroyo 1: 95, 99, 108

Asteroid 1: 10, 2: 197, 198, 199, 201, 204

Asthenosphere 1: 3–5, 17, 59, 62–64, 65 (ill.), 2: 119, 123–124, 209, 213, 3: 229, 233, 255, 257, 293, 300, 303

Aswan High Dam, Egypt 2: 139